M

Advance Praise for

The Great Neighborhood Book

There may have been a time when this kind of information was intuitive, but not
in our individualist and over-busy age. Jay Walljasper has given us nothing less
than a manual for how to rebuild community, one practical step at a time, and
in the process recover much of the joy of day-to-day life. What a gift!

— Bill McKibben, author of
Deep Economy: The Wealth of Communities and the Durable Future

We're often told that regular people have no power anymore. But when they get
together with their neighbors to work on important issues in their own backyard,
anything is possible. Jay Walljasper regales us with stories of folks all over the
country who have rolled up their sleeves to make big changes to their neighborhood
— and the world. So, read on, get riled up, roll up your sleeves...and take power!

— Jim Hightower, author of *Thieves in High Places*, and
The Hightower Lowdown

Here's a Declaration of Independence for America's neighborhoods.
It shows how it hardly matters how rich or poor you are, or whether City Hall
recognizes your zip code or not. The building blocks for great place-making
are revealed and explained — for you to build on.

— Neal Peirce, Citistates Group and Washington Post Writers Group

This is a very significant book — informative, upbeat, extremely useful and
beautifully illustrated with pictures worth a thousand words. It clearly shows how
small things can make a big difference and jump5tart significant change.

— Roberta Brandes Gratz, author, "Cities Back From the Edge:
New Life for Downtown" and "The Living City: Thinking Small in a Big Way."

With each passing day our world becomes more urban and our cities grow larger.
It is therefore ever more important that we focus more intensely and with greater
energy on the smallest parts of our cities, our neighborhoods, where our citizens
live and where their lives are shaped. The *Great Neighborhood Book* is a treasure.
It will positively influence neighborhoods in small towns to great cities throughout
our world and thereby enhance the lives of their citizens. Every city's goal should
be to have its neighborhoods inspirational and nourishing communities.
The Great Neighborhood Book will help all who care about their towns
and cities make their neighborhoods more special places.

— Mayor Joe Riley of Charleston, SC

The
Great Neighborhood
A Do-it-Yourself Guide
to Placemaking Book

The
Great Neighborhood

A Do-it-Yourself Guide
to Placemaking **Book**

JAY WALLJASPER

Success story sidebars by Benjamin Fried

All photographs by Project for Public Spaces unless otherwise noted

A Project for Public Spaces book

NEW SOCIETY PUBLISHERS

Cataloging in Publication Data:
A catalog record for this publication is available from the National Library of Canada.

Cover design by Diane McIntosh. Photos: Project for Public Spaces, Inc. Page design & layout: Carly Clark, Greg Green, Mary Jane Jessen. Printed in Canada.

First printing March 2007.

Paperback ISBN: 978-0-86571-581-3

Inquiries regarding requests to reprint all or part of *The Great Neighborhood Book* should be addressed to New Society Publishers at the address below.

To order directly from the publishers, please call toll-free (North America) 1-800-567-6772, or order online at www.newsociety.com

Any other inquiries can be directed by mail to:

New Society Publishers
P.O. Box 189, Gabriola Island, BC
V0R 1X0, Canada
1-800-567-6772

New Society Publishers' mission is to publish books that contribute in fundamental ways to building an ecologically sustainable and just society, and to do so with the least possible impact on the environment, in a manner that models this vision. We are committed to doing this not just through education, but through action. We are acting on our commitment to the world's remaining ancient forests by phasing out our paper supply from ancient forests worldwide. This book is one step toward ending global deforestation and climate change. It is printed on acid-free paper that is **100% old growth forest-free** (100% post-consumer recycled), processed chlorine free, and printed with vegetable-based, low-VOC inks. For further information, or to browse our full list of books and purchase securely, visit our website at: www.newsociety.com

NEW SOCIETY PUBLISHERS   www.newsociety.com

For all local heroes everywhere
who are changing the world by making
a difference in their neighborhoods.

Contents

Acknowledgments

It's important to offer grateful appreciation to all the folks who offered suggestions through the Project for Public Spaces website and on-line newsletter, *Making Places*. The book is richer and more diverse for their efforts. Not all their wisdom could make it into these pages, but keep watch at www.pps.org, where we plan to supplement the ideas here with new brainstorms from our readers.

It's also a pleasure to thank Dan Burden of Walkable Communities, Inc. and the people who sent terrific suggestions through his listserv. And Mimi Gates of the Seattle Art Museum deserves recognition for helping clarify the idea of the "Power of Ten."

All the staff at Project for Public Spaces put their heads together, drawing on years of experience in grassroots communities all over the world, to come up with winning strategies for making great neighborhoods.

This book represents a team effort between PPS staff and the author, Jay Walljasper. PPS took the majority of photographs, researched many of the stories, and is developing ideas for how to make this book part of a broader effort to improve neighborhoods.

Special thanks to Maija Merimaa for her indefatigable basic research; to Will Sherman for his relentless help in collecting images; to Elly Goetz for her tireless cataloging; and to Carly Clark for her impressive talent in visual presentation.

Kudos of the highest order to Benjamin Fried, who wrote all the "success story" sidebars; to Kathy Madden, who was a font of splendid ideas and who masterfully kept everything on track: and to Sandy Pan, who was good-natured, thorough, organized and nothing less than heroic on this project every step of the way.

And a hearty salute to Andy Wiley-Schwartz, who had an inspired idea for a book.

Small parts of this book first appeared in a different form in *Ode* magazine, the *Utne Reader*, and *The Nation*.

Preface

A neighborhood love story

The idea that vital neighborhoods play a huge role in enhancing our lives first struck me, ironically, a long way from home. My wife Julie and I spent a week in Paris on our honeymoon, arriving with big plans to cover every inch of the city, from the modern towers of La Défense to the immigrant quarters of Rue du Faubourg du Temple. Yet we found ourselves passing entire days within just a few blocks of our hotel on the Left Bank. We'd stroll the boulevards, buy lunch in a street market, watch Parisians enjoying themselves in Luxembourg Gardens, and while away hours in sidewalk cafés. We agreed that the Pompidou Centre and Versailles could wait for another trip. We were immersed in the life of our "village."

Back home in Minneapolis, when it came time to buy a house, Julie and I sought a place that offered a similar feel, even if it was a Midwestern tavern on the corner rather than a Parisian bistro. The problem was that many other folks had the same idea, and all the neighborhoods that attracted us as "urban villages" were out of our price range. So we stayed put in a one-bedroom apartment in the bustling Uptown district for more than four years.

Finally, we fell in love with a 1914 craftsman-style house with lots of sunlight and took the plunge. Our new neighborhood, Kingfield, was pleasant, with tree-lined streets and well-built homes, but the noticeable lack of street life made moving there feel a little like exile. Luckily, we soon fell in with a group of neighbors, mostly newcomers like us, who got together on Friday nights for potluck suppers and enthusiastic conversation. We would swap stories about backyard gardens and remodeling projects as well as our wishes for more places to go and things to do in Kingfield. We also compared notes on the nagging crime problem.

All these discussions eventually led us to become involved with the local neighborhood organization, which, much to our surprise, was often uncooperative to people wanting to open new businesses in the area. The neighborhood board also refused to take a stand against the widening of an already busy street in the neighborhood, which would threaten safety and property values.

That was all it took to make neighborhood activists out of us. We recruited a slate of candidates to run for the board, talked to everyone about the issues that concerned us, and swept to victory. Julie became the new neighborhood board president, and most of our potluck friends joined in various efforts to revitalize the community. We showed up at numerous public meetings to voice support for proposals and policies we felt were important for our neighborhood. Citizen safety initiatives and community policing programs tackled the crime problem. The street-widening proposal was beaten back, thanks to work by people across many neighborhoods. I joined a city task force charged with suggesting plans to calm the traffic on Lyndale Avenue, the street once scheduled for widening.

We have seen the neighborhood gradually change. It bears a much closer resemblance to the kind of place Julie and I had dreamed about living. Kingfield now sports a farmer market, a performing arts center, good restaurants with sidewalk tables, new energy in the business districts, new streetscapes, housing improvements in its low-income blocks, and a growing sense of local pride. As our son Soren (who spent much of his early years bouncing on various people's knees at numerous public meetings) grows older, we spend more time at soccer games and school events, but a new wave of impassioned neighbors are continuing the push to make our neighborhood great — and we pitch in to help. I now tell people I live in Kingfield, rather than "someplace south of Uptown."

This first-hand experience in what Project for Public Spaces (PPS) calls "Placemaking"

(although I didn't learn the term until years later) instilled us with a strong sense that people have the power to make a difference in their neighborhoods. Julie, Soren, and I can now stroll around the corner to Caffe Tempo for a croissant or dessert — something that's possible only because we and dozens of neighbors spoke our minds at a zoning variance meeting. And I can't wait for this summer when the construction crews descend upon Lyndale Avenue, once slated for widening, to carry out our citizens' plan to narrow the street, making it more attractive and safer.

This book is full of similar examples from communities large and small across the continent. When people get together with neighbors to solve a problem or pursue a goal, almost anything is possible. That's because — as PPS always says — the people who live in a particular locale are the experts on that place. As neighbors, you possess the wisdom and vision to make your neighborhood great. It's simpler than you think, more fun than you can imagine, and will improve your life in profound ways.

Introduction

Changing the world one place at a time

The neighborhood is the basic unit of human civilization. Unlike cities, counties, wards, townships, enterprise zones, and other artificial entities, the neighborhood is easily recognizable as a real place. It's the spot on earth we call home. It's where our lives unfold day after day — meeting friends at the coffee shop, chatting with neighbors on the street, going about our business in stores, parks, gathering spots, and our own backyard. Some people may be indifferent to events in their city, or even the nation, but fiercely engaged in their neighborhood because what happens there affects them in direct, personal ways.

Neighborhoods — whether in cities, suburbs, or small towns — are the level of social organization at which people interact most regularly and naturally, providing a ready-made forum for tackling problems that arise in a community. Even in places where there are no pressing troubles, the neighborhood remains the ideal setting for getting important things done, like restoring a park, enlivening a business district, or boosting the sense of community.

At their best, neighborhoods function as villages, in which residents' lives overlap in positive ways. We look out for one another and share a public life in common. Everyone who wants to change the world, or simply make improvements in their own lives, is well advised to sit down with the neighbors

and work together to make their dreams come true. You'll be surprised what can be accomplished if you are willing to think big about your little place in the world.

PPS was founded in 1975 with the mission of helping people bring new life to their neighborhoods. Drawing on the ideas of civic visionaries like William H. Whyte and Jane Jacobs, we at PPS are committed to helping communities find the tools they need to improve their business districts, parks, streets, squares, community centers and other public places. Over the past 32 years, working in more than 2,000 communities in 26 countries, we have continually witnessed the amazing power of everyday citizens to change their world.

Many cities and towns around the world have recently experienced remarkable turnarounds due in large part to "local heroes" who have introduced new ideas and brought new energy to their communities. Sometimes they are fixing a problem on a certain street corner, at other times masterminding the revival of an entire downtown; but in every case these citizen-led efforts set the stage for more improvements to come.

When it comes to revitalizing communities, the importance of the average citizen cannot be overestimated. That's the reason we created *The Great Neighborhood Book* — to highlight the success stories of everyday people that can inspire you to do similar things in your own communities. Some folks start with a simple idea, like putting a bench in front of their house for neighbors who want to rest and socialize (see page 11). Others directly address fear in their communities, like Jutta Mason in Toronto, who pulled together a group of neighbors, including teenagers thought of as the local "toughs," to bring life back to a local park (see page 127). Still others act as catalysts for the rebirth of a district, like Dana Crawford, who saved a block of historic buildings in Denver's Larimer Square and created a new heart in the city (see page 169).

What these citizens have in common is that they are, in the best sense of the phrase, "zealous nuts" — meaning they are dedicated to making their communities better places. They usually have a strong intuitive sense of what makes neighborhoods safe, lively, prosperous, and interesting. They know more about their communities than any designers or other self-proclaimed experts because they live and work there, which gives them insight on what needs to be done and the best ways to make it happen. Zealous nuts make sure the places we live are loved and well cared for. No lasting progress in any town or city ever happens without the involvement of these "local heroes." It's as simple as that.

Talk with any zealous nut and you will find them open and more than happy to share the secrets of their success, which often follows a pattern like this:

First, they become aware of a problem, which they see diminishing the quality of life in their neighborhood.

Then they recognize that they can't wait for the authorities in government or other institutions to do anything about it because their neighborhood's concerns will likely be perceived as too small or parochial, too controversial, not in keeping with the normal ways of doing business, or not fitting neatly into the responsibilities of any one department.

Next, they shape a general vision for what needs to be done, whether it is slowing traffic so their children can cross the street, saving old buildings to maintain the character of their community, or getting to know their neighbors. Sometimes they discover that they can make change happen very quickly by acting on their own.

In some cases, they launch a public campaign, making alliances with others who are experiencing the same problem and finding a way to communicate their ideas to the entire community.

In working with neighborhoods of all types throughout the world — big city and small town; prosperous and poor; recently built and centuries old — we've noticed one thing that usually sets a great neighborhood apart from a mediocre one

— there are a wealth of good places in great neighborhoods where people can relax, have fun, and meet up with one another. Here are four basic characteristics that make a good place:

Good places promote sociability. These are the spots where you run into people you know. They are the places you take friends and family when you want to show them the neighborhood. They become the center of the action by offering people many different reasons to go there.

Good places offer lots of things to do. The places we love most are the ones where we can pursue a variety of activities. Without opportunities to do something more than sit and look, the experience you have in that place is "thin" — there is nothing to keep you there for any length of time.

Good places are comfortable and attractive. They beckon you to walk through and maybe stay a while. Flowers, comfortable benches with nice views, and attractive lighting all make you feel this is the place you want to be. In contrast, a place that lacks these types of amenities often feels unwelcoming or has a bad image. It may be unsafe or just feel unsafe, but either way, you don't want to stay there.

Good places are accessible. These places are clearly identifiable from a distance, easy to enter when you get closer, and simple to use. A space that is not accessible will end up empty, forlorn, and often neglected or dilapidated.

Throughout years of work all over the world, we have learned key lessons about what makes a place thrive — a process that we have come to call "Placemaking."

Here are the 11 principles of Placemaking:

1. **The community is the expert.** The people living and working in a place are the folks who know what needs to be done and how best to do it.

2. **You are creating a place, not a design.** The blueprints for a neighborhood improvement effort are much less critical to its success than other factors, such as a management plan and the involvement of local citizens.

3. **You can't do it alone.** Finding the right partners will bring more resources, innovative ideas, and new sources of energy for your efforts.

4. **They'll always say "It can't be done."** When government officials, business people, and even some of your own neighbors say it won't work, what they really mean is "We've never done it like this before." It's a sign you're on the right track.

5. **You can see a lot by just observing.** The smartest way to turn a neighborhood around is to first take a close look at what goes on there,

watching out for what works and what doesn't in that particular place.

6. **Develop a vision.** For a community vision to make sense and to make a difference, it needs to come from the people who live there, not from consultants or other outside professionals.

7. **Form supports function.** If you don't take into account how people use a particular place in the beginning, you will have to deal with the consequences later.

8. **Make the connections.** A great place in a neighborhood offers many things to do, all of which enhance each other and add up to more than the sum of the parts.

9. **Start with petunias.** Little things can set the stage for big changes, especially by proving to local skeptics that change is indeed possible.

10. **Money is not the issue.** If you have a spirited community working with you, you'll find creative ways around financial obstacles.

11. **You are never finished.** Eighty percent of the success of any good place is due to how well it is managed after the project is done.

How many good places does your neighborhood need? In all of our work, PPS asks people to identify the most important places in their region, in their city or town, and in their neighborhoods.

We then ask them to think about the number of things there are to do in each of these places. Cumulatively, the quality of life in any locale will grow exponentially if each place within it is good and offers at least ten interesting and distinct things to do there. We have come to call this idea the Power of Ten, based on Charles Eames' concept and our discussions with Mimi Gates of the Seattle Art Museum, for the universal way it applies to every neighborhood or community.

Think about your own region for a minute and write down the ten most important places that are nearby — these are the spots you frequently go or recommend to others. These places could be an especially charming village, a major park, a historic district, etc. Now think about your city or town and identify the ten most important places there. It could be your main street, the riverfront, an interesting shop, a library, museum, post office, etc. Zoom in and think about one of these places and try to write down the smaller places that make up that place. For example, if you named the main street as an important place, what are the little places on that street where you enjoy spending time? You can shop there, of course, but if your main street is truly a good place, you can also sit outside on a bench and talk to your neighbors, get a cup of coffee nearby, and enjoy the passing scene.

There are literally thousands of possibilities you can draw on in your efforts to create good places in your neighborhood. Here is a small sampling of improvements that can make a big impact, based on ideas detailed in this book:

Create a strong sense of community by putting a bench out in front of your house where people can stop to sit and chat with each other.

Tame traffic in neighborhoods by making streets so interesting that people naturally slow down to see what is going on.

Develop new activities for teens that make them want to get involved in the future of their neighborhood instead of feeling excluded and alienated from the community.

Introduce new kinds of park activities, such as gardens catering to certain groups — for example, children, seniors, or various ethnic groups — or a bread oven that is used to cook community dinners.

Improve safety and security in a neighborhood by encouraging people to do things like saying hello to everyone they see. This can change the spirit of a community faster and more effectively than a police presence will ever do.

Bring new kinds of people downtown with creative campaigns that deliver social and economic benefits for these critical core neighborhoods.

Promote new opportunities for social interaction and community pride by introducing activities from different cultures, such as bocce ball courts, casitas, or an evening promenade.

Make kids healthier by developing innovative programs so they can safely walk or bike to school once again.

Establish more effective community-based planning processes that result in less arguing, more public input, and a general level of agreement on what to do to make the community better.

Foster new types of businesses that not only make money but also have more far-reaching impacts — for example, rent fun and unique bikes to people who don't ordinarily ride bikes, like seniors, disabled people, and young children.

Champion your local hangout by making it a "Third Place." Every vital neighborhood needs what sociologist Ray Oldenburg calls a "Third Place" — a coffee shop, café or other spot where everyone feels welcome and can strike up a conversation with their neighbors. Starbucks, whose mission was inspired by Oldenburg, built its business this way. Its phenomenal growth has helped spark a boom in locally owned coffee shops all over the world.

Provide clean public restrooms through enterprising programs that grow out of partnerships between businesses and the downtown association. The big question is, of course, how do you begin to create the good places that every neighborhood craves? What process can you use to build places where people want to hang out? Long experience has shown us that bottom-up strategies work better than top-down approaches. The bottom-up strategy recognizes citizens as the experts, is guided by the wisdom of the community, and builds a strong partnership between the public and private sectors.

This is the most important thing we've learned in the more than 30 years we've been working to make great neighborhoods.

We are inspired over and over by the commitment, vision, and warmth of the zealous nuts we meet. They truly are local heroes, and we tell many of their stories in this book. But there are thousands more stories that we couldn't fit in. Each neighborhood is different, yet local heroes all share the passion, patience, and love necessary to make their communities better. We applaud them all, and everyone else who is making the world a little better by improving their small piece of it.

We want to hear your neighborhood stories

Tell us what worked to improve your own community. Post your stories and photos on the Great Neighborhoods discussion forum at www.pps.org:

or send to:

Neighborhood Success Stories, c/o PPS, 700 Broadway, 4th Floor, New York, NY 10003.

Be sure to include contact information so we can reach you and anyone else involved with the project. We are compiling success stories for future projects and books. For more information see www.pps.org.

The citizen takes his city for granted far too often.
He forgets to marvel.

— *Carlos Fuentes, Mexican novelist*

It's really wonderful to wake up in a city where every day you realize
that today the city is a little bit better than yesterday.

— *Jan Gehl, Danish architect*

I believe very strongly that the cities that pay attention
— really pay attention — to quality of life will be
the cities that thrive in the 21st century.

— *Richard M. Daley, Chicago mayor*

A society grows great when old men plant trees whose shade
they know they shall never sit in.

— *Greek proverb*

The revolution starts now
In your own backyard
In your own hometown

— *Steve Earle, Nashville singer-songwriter*

Chapter 1

Feeling Right at Home

How to foster a sense of community

 Smile. Wave. Greet everyone.

 Spark a revival of old-fashioned neighborliness

 Give yourself a break

 Go for a stroll

 Look at familiar places with fresh eyes

 Don't bowl alone

 Be bold in introducing yourself

 Let your neighborhood go to the dogs

 Sing along

 Organize your block

 Get your daily dose of vitamin T

Smile. Wave. Greet Everyone.

It's more important than you could ever imagine

It couldn't be more simple: great neighborhoods are friendly neighborhoods. A smiling face, laughter in the air, a hearty hello can make all the difference between a good day and a dull, disappointing day. Humans evolved as social creatures, and the chance to exchange greetings with acquaintances, or even strangers, makes us feel happy and safe.

David Burwell, a long-time environmental lawyer and PPS senior associate in Washington, DC, has been tracking recent research from the field of evolutionary biology. He believes that, as a species, we are hardwired to seek convivial public settings where we can comfortably connect with one another. In fact, these kinds of places are essential to the future of the human species because they're where boys and girls have always gone to meet one another, flirt, and, eventually, mate.

David Engwicht, an Australian activist and a leading spokesman for traffic calming, takes this idea even further. Human civilization developed, he says, from an endless series of spontaneous exchanges between people. The more opportunities there are for exchanges, he theorizes, the more rich and satisfying life is for people in that society.

Many wonder today if we're in danger of losing these primal, civilizing instincts. The harried, isolating nature of modern life appears to be minimizing our capacity for human contact. D. Jean Hester created an art project in which she greeted everyone she met in the Central Square neighborhood of Cambridge, Massachusetts, and the results were alarming — most people responded with icy stares or nasty looks. Student journalist Mani O'Brien offers a bit more hope. She conducted a similar experiment around Tempe, Arizona, and found that she elicited positive reactions with a laid-back and cheerful "hi" but not with a cool "hello."

So make it your mission to spread a little cheer all around. You may improve more than your neighborhood; you might help save human civilization.

RESOURCES

D. Jean Hester: "Hello"
www.glowlab.com

David Engwicht:
www.lesstraffic.com

A great neighborhood is a friendly neighborhood.

DAVE MARCUCCI

The bench that built a community

Mississauga, Ontario, Canada

It doesn't take much to start a public space renaissance in your neighborhood. In fact, as Dave Marcucci discovered, a simple bench can do the trick. After attending a PPS training course in 2005, Marcucci came away inspired by the idea that every neighborhood should have ten great places. He returned home to Mississauga, Ontario, determined to make his house, which occupies a prime corner lot, one of the great places in his neighborhood.

Marcucci started by tearing out the fence at the corner of his front yard. As he got to work landscaping the area and constructing a bench, he received a lot of quizzical comments. "Why don't you build a bench for yourself in the backyard?" He would answer, "The bench is for you."

When the bench was finished, Marcucci threw a street party. Soon, everyone in the neighborhood was coming by to sit on the bench. Older people stop to rest on it during their evening strolls. Kids sit there as they wait for the school bus in the morning. Families out for a walk use it to take a breather.

The complications that Marcucci first anticipated have not come to pass. The bench has not been vandalized, nor has it attracted negative uses. It was installed without approval from the city, but no one has demanded to see a permit.

"There have been no problems!" he exclaims. "It's worked out really well. I've met my neighbors and other people I'd never met before. It's added a really friendly atmosphere to the neighborhood. You sit on the bench, and as people walk by, they stop and talk to you!"

The bench is so popular that a homeowner around the corner from Marcucci has added his own bench for the whole neighborhood to use.

By adding a bench to his front yard, Dave Marcucci gave folks a congenial gathering spot in suburban Toronto.

Spark a Revival of Old-Fashioned Neighborliness

How busy people can reach out to those who need a little help

In our grandparents' time it would have been unthinkable not to take a casserole over to the family down the block coping with an illness, a death, or a colicky baby.

Nowadays that seems the stuff of fairy tales. As nice as it would be, everyone's too busy to take on those sorts of duties. Besides, we're not as close to our neighbors as we were in the 1940s or '50s. One wonders what happened to the tight-knit communities we pine for when watching reruns of *Leave It to Beaver* or *The Honeymooners*. But friendly, nurturing neighborhoods didn't just magically happen in the good old days. They were the result of conscious effort, usually carried out by women.

Even with many women working outside the home today, there's no reason the folks on your block can't do the kind of good deeds that turn folks-next-door into friends. People have less time now, of course, but we can compensate with e-mail, computer programs, and other efficiently modern tools. Chart out how everyone can take turns doing yard work and household errands for older people or strapped single parents. Divvy up who brings dinner to those who need it — and remember it's quite all right to simply pick up something scrumptious at the deli.

Parents in the Kingfield neighborhood of Minneapolis maintain a babysitting co-op that lets them give each other a break from looking after the kids. For every hour they help out another family, they log an hour that they can redeem for childcare for their own kids. Such arrangements are common in many places throughout the United States and Canada.

In Hyattsville, Maryland, an electronic mailing list (listserv) has become the talk of the town thanks to a group called Hyattsville Organization for a Positive Environment (HOPE). People post messages about everything, from a lost-dog notice to well-researched critiques on development proposals for Route 1 outside town. A couple of hundred people, including public officials, closely monitor the opinions and discussions on-line, which means that things get done. A safety fence between a roaring highway and a nearby shopping area was built as a direct result of conversations on the listserv.

You could easily do the same for your town, neighborhood, or block, getting the word out on everything from a progressive dinner party to crime prevention.

Devoted fans of the old movie *It's a Wonderful Life* will remember the scene in which an immigrant family moving into a new home in Bedford Falls receives a loaf of bread and bottle of wine from George Bailey. That's another old tradition well worth reviving. Set up an ad hoc welcoming committee to formally greet your new neighbors, and fix a date after they've settled in to meet for coffee or drinks with the whole block. In the Bungalow Heaven neighborhood of Pasadena, California, newcomers are greeted with a packet of information on neighborhood history (including the background on their own house), happenings, and local resources.

These are the kinds of small investments that pay big dividends through the creation of a rich sense of community.

RESOURCES
Babysitting co-ops:
    www.todaysparent.com
Hyattsville Organization for a
    Positive Environment listserv:
    groups.yahoo.com/group/
    HOPE_in_Hyattsville/

A game of dominoes is part of the glue that holds a community together in Havana, Cuba.

Give Yourself a Break

Slow down and enjoy what's most satisfying about your neighborhood

The greatest threat to community life is the frantic, harried, out-of-control, supersonic, unbelievably crazy pace of life that afflicts so many of us today.

You can live in the greatest neighborhood in the universe, but if you can't take the time to stop in the cozy corner coffee shop, wander over to the farmers market on Saturday morning, or chat for a minute with your neighbor in front of the grocery store, then you might as well live on the dark side of the moon. And if too many people in your neighborhood have this same kind of busy schedule, chances are things won't stay great for long.

The basic fact is that it takes time and energy to make a neighborhood lively. Someone must take on the responsibility to organize the street fair or make sure the local park remains safe and welcoming for kids. That's one of the issues behind gentrification controversies in city neighborhoods and small towns. Not only do long-time residents get priced out of their homes, but the whole spirit of the place can change as concerned citizens involved in local issues are replaced by people who move there for the prestigious address or a good real estate investment rather than the community life. The wealthier newcomers often work demanding jobs, so they've got no energy to invest in civic projects, and they may spend their free time in exotic travel or at a vacation home rather than hanging out around the neighborhood. While per capita income in the area rises, the richness of civic life declines.

Taking the time to appreciate all that's going on around you each day is one of the best investments you can make. Think twice about signing up for another class across town. You could learn a lot more exploring the streets around your home each evening. Trade the treadmill and stationary bicycle for a stroll or bike ride. Cancel your cable TV service and spend the savings at local diners and taverns, where you'll get more important news, far more interesting stories, and even more opinionated sports coverage. Whole new worlds will open up, and you'll feel more relaxed to boot.

A number of cities across Italy realized the importance a leisurely pace of life played in keeping their communities vital, so they launched a league of Slow Cities in 2000. Associated with the burgeoning Slow Food Movement, more than 100 cities (in Brazil, Norway, Sweden, Japan, Greece, Switzerland, and Great Britain as well as Italy) joined the network, united in the belief that the good life is an unhurried experience. Proudly displaying the Slow Cities logo around their towns, members pledged to:

- Restrain racing traffic by limiting automobiles and

promoting sustainable transportation alternatives such as bikes and pedestrian zones.

- Encourage businesses, schools, and government to improve the quality of life by allowing people to take time off for a long midday meal.
- Promote good food by sponsoring farmers markets and preserving local culinary traditions.
- Curtail noise pollution and visual blight by limiting car alarms, outdoor advertising, and unsightly signs.

"We are not against the modern world," explains Mayor Paolo Saturnini of Greve, a slow city in Tuscany. "We just want to protect what is good in our lives and keep our unique town character."

RESOURCES

Slow Cities:
www.cittaslow.net
www.citymayors.com/
environment/slow_cities.html

Take the time to truly appreciate what's best about your community.

Go for a Stroll

The Latin custom of an evening walk is good for you — and for the health of your neighborhood

We all know that walking is good for us. It burns calories, tones muscles, and clears our minds. The French philosopher Jean-Jacques Rousseau once confessed, "I can only meditate when I'm walking. When I stop, my mind ceases to think; my mind only works with my legs."

People living in pedestrian-friendly metropolitan areas are less likely to have chronic health conditions, such as high blood pressure and respiratory problems, than those living in areas where walking is a less common activity, according to a recent study by the RAND Corporation, a noted research firm in Santa Monica, California. But taking a regular walk is also beneficial for your neighborhood. This basic human instinct — to get out of the house to see what's going on — is the glue that holds most great communities together. The classic examples are in the warm-weather lands, where an after-dinner stroll — the *passeggiata* in Italy, the *paseo* in Spain and Latin America, the *volta* in Greece — is as much a part of the culture as sunshine or siestas. In towns and even large cities, people amble around the same set of streets each evening. The shops are usually closed, so the purpose is not shopping and errands, but to connect with neighbors and enjoy the surroundings.

American writer Adam Goodheart recounts this scene near the main square of the Italian hill town of Eboli. "I realized that I kept seeing the same people, but in different combinations. Here came a blond woman pushing a stroller. Next lap, she was arm in arm with a younger woman and the stroller was nowhere to be seen. Later, they'd been joined by an old lady who was pushing the stroller. Next, they were surrounded by men, jackets draped over their shoulders ...."

The words *passeggiata* and *paseo* translate into English as

Where the action is: Stepping out in Brighton Beach, New York.

"promenade" — and the idea translates too, according to Christopher Alexander, a former Berkeley architecture professor who has devoted his life to scientifically studying what makes places work. In his classic book *A Pattern Language* he asks, "Is the promenade in fact a purely Latin institution? Our experiments suggest that it is not ... It seems that people, of all cultures, may have a general need for this kind of human mixing which the promenade makes possible."

Two factors define the experience of a promenade, according to Alexander:

- The route should be approximately 1,500 feet, which can easily be walked in ten minutes at a leisurely pace. People may opt for many times around, especially teenagers on the lookout for excitement, but you don't want to make the course too long for kids or elderly people.
- It's important that there are things to see and do along the route, with few empty or dead zones. While the primary purpose of these strolls is social, people also like to have some destination: a sidewalk café, playground, bookstore, bar, ice-cream shop, etc.

Think about what blocks in your neighborhood show promise for strolling and what improvements could be made to encourage more people to go there. Walking up and down main street or any lively commercial district is probably the most common North American version of the promenade, although a route along a waterfront or interesting residential blocks could work just as well. Public art, welcoming businesses, benches, flowerbeds, even a vending cart could all help solidify this area as the place in your community where people go after dinner to see and be seen.

Providence, Rhode Island, has proven on a grand scale that if you build it, people will stroll. WaterFire, Barnaby Evans' flaming, water-borne sculpture installation, has turned the downtown riverfront into a popular promenade. On nights WaterFire is lit, the human traffic is so plentiful that local authorities advise everyone to walk counterclockwise between the Staples Street bridge and a nearby pedestrian bridge to minimize crowding. The project, which runs May to September thanks to hundreds of volunteers, has been credited with revitalizing downtown Providence.

RESOURCES

A Pattern Language by Christopher Alexander (Oxford University Press, 1977)

WaterFire Providence: www.waterfire.org

Checking out the excitement in Market Square, Pittsburgh, Pennsylvania.

Look at Familiar Places with Fresh Eyes

A simple change of habit lets you see the neighborhood in a new light

The great American poet T.S. Eliot once remarked that the true value of travel is in coming home so we can "arrive where we started / And know the place for the first time." A change of scenery is great for reminding us what we like and don't like about our hometowns, but it's also possible — and a whole lot cheaper — to get a fresh look at where we live through a simple change of habits.

Break out of your rut, for instance, by taking the train or bus to a place you would usually drive. You'll see new people and experience your community in unexpected ways. Or when you are running around town, trade your usual seat in the car, bus, or train for a bicycle. A whole new world of side streets will open up, with blooming gardens, kids frolicking on the sidewalks, and curious corners of the neighborhood you never noticed.

Even better is leaving the car or bike at home and hoofing it. You'll be moving at the speed of life, transforming an ordinary trip into an architectural, botanical, cultural, and sociological adventure. (If you live in a spread-out community with long distances to cover, try parking a few blocks from your destination and exploring the new territory in between.) You'll discover all sorts of wonders that most folks miss, like enterprising seven-year-olds selling lemonade, or religious and artistic shrines tucked away in side yards.

Francine Corcoran, 55, took this idea quite a few steps farther by walking every single block in her hometown of Minneapolis — a 1,071-mile odyssey that took three years. Word of her project spread thanks to a newspaper story, and she heard from people who have done the same thing in New York City, San Francisco, and Christchurch, New Zealand.

The late urban visionary Jane Jacobs stressed that simply observing what goes on around you is the best method of determining what needs to be improved (and what doesn't) around the neighborhood. So start your research right now.

RESOURCE

The Death and Life of Great American Cities by Jane Jacobs (Random House, 1961)

This garden raises hopes as well as vegetables

Philadelphia, Pennsylvania

Las Parcelas, a group of inter-connected vacant lots in the West Kensington neighborhood, was once considered the drug capital of North Philadelphia. Dealers would sell from abandoned cars and hide drugs for pickup in vacant lots, while drug users from throughout the region congregated in the neighborhood park. A group of neighbors who cared deeply for their community started working with the police to push the dealers out. As part of their efforts they envisioned a new and exciting future for Las Parcelas.

The vacant lots became the core of a neighborhood revitalization effort coordinated by the local organization Philadelphia Green. Volunteers turned Las Parcelas into a beautiful community garden. And they didn't stop there. The women in the neighborhood said the garden wasn't enough; they wanted Las Parcelas to have an outdoor community kitchen and to represent the neighborhood's strong Puerto Rican heritage. They worked with Philadelphia Green to build a *casita*, a one-room house filled with small objects of special significance in Puerto Rican culture. And they painted a mural on a wall beside the garden, full of bright lavenders, yellows, oranges, and blues.

What was once a terrible blight has been transformed into a place that embodies history, tradition, and promise. Today people go to Las Parcelas to cook, play dominoes, drum, and dance. "When people come together to transform a neglected park or vacant parcel, their focus is on the land, but somehow more than just the land is changed," says Joan Reilly of Philadelphia Green. "We all become transformed in the process. Las Parcelas is a wonderful illustration of this truth. That is the power of placemaking."

RESOURCE
Philadelphia Green & Las Parcelas: www.pennsylvaniahorticultural society.org

Growing vegetables has replaced dealing drugs at many vacant lots in North Philadelphia, much to the relief of local residents.

Don't Bowl Alone

Civic organizations — from church groups to volunteer fire departments — may not be fashionable, but they're the lifeblood of our communities

Harvard sociologist Robert Putnam got the shock of his life in Italy. He was studying the quality of public services offered in different regions and assumed, like everyone else, that the richer the region, the better its public services. What he discovered, however, was that it wasn't economic wealth but community wealth that made a difference. The regions of Italy that had the strongest civic organizations — everything from musical societies and soccer clubs to unions and cooperatives — also enjoyed the best government services and social harmony. When people get together for any reason, Putnam concluded, good things happen far beyond the narrow scope of the group.

Shifting his attention to the United States, Putnam grew worried about what he found. Long-standing civic organizations were losing members as people felt too busy to get involved in their communities. For Putnam, bowling became the symbol of all this. More people than ever were going bowling, but they were doing it in atomized groups of two or four. Bowling leagues, where the same people get together on the same night every week, thereby creating strong social bonds, were declining. And the vitality of American communities was declining along with them.

Putnam published a famous article, "Bowling Alone," that was expanded into a book in which he articulated his theory that communities need social capital (the investments ordinary people make by putting time into local organizations) as much as they need economic capital (the investments banks and businesses make by putting money into neighborhoods).

When you roll up your sleeves to make improvements in your neighborhood or town, look around a moment to make sure you're not reinventing the wheel. Might the energy consumed in your plans for a new project be better spent bringing some new blood and a fresh direction to an existing group — the local PTA or Lions Club, a business improvement association or community education program, a neighborhood organization or network of religious congregations, a youth sports league, a church choir, an emergency food shelf, or the library board? You might be surprised at what's already going on.

In Wauwatosa, Wisconsin, a suburb of Milwaukee, the Olde Hillcrest Neighborhood Association sponsors a community book club where neighbors can, according to the group's website, "get together with fellow book enthusiasts to converse, discuss and debate current bestsellers and classics alike." And, of course, get to know each other better. There is even a special parent/child book club. The organization also sponsors a children's playgroup, a craft club, two different personal finance clubs, a seniors' activity group, a helping hands group that reaches out to neighbors with special needs, and a women's Bunko club (the club's website explains that Bunko is an "easy to learn" dice game).

Of course, it may turn out that an entirely new organization best suits your purposes. While Veterans of Foreign Wars or Knights of Columbus halls are usually full of lively discussion, they may not be the ideal setting to explore certain subjects, such as how to bring about environmental sustainability in the neighborhood or promote world peace. (Although you never know — in 2006 the Knights of Columbus took out an ad in the *New York Times* asking everyone to pray for peace.)

Tom Sander, executive director of the Saguaro Seminar, a program of Harvard's John F. Kennedy School of Government that promotes civic engagement, says these kinds of civic organizations — both old and new — make community connections that are "crucial to schools working well, neighborhoods being safe, economies working well ...."

RESOURCES

Robert Putnam:
   www.bettertogether.org
Saguaro Seminar at Harvard's
   John F. Kennedy School of
   Government:
   www.ksg.harvard.edu/saguaro

Bowling Alone: The Collapse and Revival of American Community by Robert D. Putnam (Simon & Schuster, 2000)

Better Together: Restoring the American Community by Robert D. Putnam and Lewis M. Feldstein with Don Cohen (Simon & Schuster, 2003)

Olde Hillcrest Neighborhood
   Association:
   www.oldehillcrest.org

There is power in numbers, as volunteers in Dade City, Florida, proudly show.

DADE CITY GARDEN CLUB

Eric Higbee (City Repair)

How a lowly intersection became a vibrant public square

Portland, Oregon

When is an intersection more than just two streets coming together? In Portland's Sellwood neighborhood, a prominent inter-section also serves as a central plaza with a community bulletin board, kids' playhouse, food stand, and 24-hour tea station. The redesigned intersection, which is painted in bright colors, came about because the community wanted to create a place with a "Main Street" feel close to home. Known as "Share-It Square" (a play on Sherrett Street, which intersects with Southeast 9th Avenue to make the plaza), the intersection was improved by neighborhood residents with assistance from a local nonprofit called the City Repair Project.

City Repair calls this process, in which residents work together to generate ideas for turning streets into public squares, "intersection repair." Thanks to a new city ordinance that passed with the help of City Repair, this kind of project can go forward if 80 percent of the people within a two-block radius of an intersection consent. People may choose to do an intersection repair because they want a place for community interaction and seasonal celebra-tions, or simply because they want to slow traffic. The only costs are paint and other mate-rials needed, which must be financed by the community.

Intersection repairs vary from neighborhood to neighborhood. One community may decide to paint a giant mural on the inter-section and stop there. Another may go through many phases: painting the street, installing a community bulletin board, building a mini-café on a corner, reconstructing the intersection with brick and cobblestones, opening businesses to make it a village center. The results can be dramatic. After installation of Share-It Square, a survey revealed that more than 85 per-cent of residents felt that crime had decreased, traffic had slowed, and communication between neighbors had improved.

RESOURCE
City Repair Project:
  www.cityrepair.org

A bright painting of a ladybug in a street in Wallingford, Seattle, has turned an ordinary inter-section into a lively destination.

By complete accident, we at PPS were reminded of the value of places where everyone knows your name. We offer regular *How to Turn a Place Around* workshops that train policy-makers and neighborhood activists in new strategies to improve their communities. These workshops attract people from all over the world, many of whom are first-time visitors to New York, and some confess a little anxiety about finding their way around such a big city.

At a recent workshop at our office, which is right in the heart of Greenwich Village, we offered attendees the chance to go out and explore one of the world's most fascinating neighborhoods. Several of the more nervous visitors returned with big grins on their faces, remarking on how friendly everyone was. They had forgotten to remove the nametags from their shirts and jackets, and people up and down the avenues greeted them by their first names. Several New Yorkers asked where they were from and happily offered suggestions on what to see and where to eat. One enterprising panhandler even adapted his usual spiel: "Hi, Lisa, how are you? Enjoying your trip to New York? I was wondering if you have any spare change."

That got us thinking about how nametags are a practical tool for communities everywhere. The mayor or community leaders (or even you and a few friends) could pick a date to hand out nametags for everyone in the neighborhood to wear. You can easily find the usual "Hello I'm _____" tags from the office supply store, or maybe commission handmade tags from kids in the neighborhood or other budding artists.

Imagine wearing your nametag at the grocery store, in the park, while walking down the street. It could launch a dozen conversations with people you often see but don't know. You'll suddenly be on a first-name basis with the guy you always see at the coffee shop (Ivan), the mother who waits every day at the bus stop to pick up her daughter (Vicki and little Lateesha), the young couple who moved onto the next block (Brett and Maria). And names are just the beginning. Soon you'll know their stories, too, and the world will seem a little friendlier.

RESOURCE
How to Turn a Place Around workshops: www.pps.org

Be Bold in Introducing Yourself

All you need is a nametag

Hello, my name is …

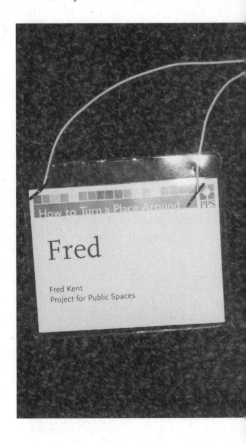

When dogs meet on the street, like these Chicago pooches, so do people.

Let Your Neighborhood Go to the Dogs

Anywhere pets thrive, people will thrive too

Even if you don't own a dog or cat, it's in your best interest to make sure the community is congenial to four-legged neighbors. Why? Because places that cater to pets and pet owners are generally safer, stable, and more vital.

Pets need the same things we do in order to thrive: safe and lively streets, parks and open spaces, places to hang out. Dogs, especially, are an indicator species for urban livability. From fancy Afghan hounds to scrappy mutts, all of them look forward to their daily walk with boundless enthusiasm. If there is no hospitable place for a stroll, the dogs in your neighborhood won't be happy — and neither will most humans. A healthy population of happy dogs, on the other hand, means that you will have dog owners strolling the sidewalks at all hours — the best recipe to prevent crime and promote a sense of community.

Kay Cavagnaro, a community organizer in San Francisco's Golden Gate Heights neighborhood, says walking dogs is the best way for people to get to know one another. A favorite hangout in her part of town, according to the *San Francisco Chronicle,* is the sidewalk in front of Golden Gate Video at 10th and Noriega, where many dog owners meet up every evening on their walks. The video store owner, Vince Palmini, welcomes them all, saying it's good for business.

Tapping the dog-owner market can be a winning strategy for many local businesses. Many stores and coffee shops offer free doggie treats, set out water dishes, and provide secure places to tie dogs up. Indeed, a relaxed attitude about bringing pets into the shop or café, which is commonly done in Europe, would be a boost for both business and neighborhood spirit. The health department doesn't have to know. (You could even challenge these sorts of archaic health regulations, as people questioned equally misguided bans on sidewalk cafés a generation ago.)

As North American households shrink in size due to divorce, fewer couples having children, and other social trends, pets play an increasingly significant role as companions in many people's lives. Four out of ten US households now have a dog. If your community doesn't seem friendly to pets, you may find that fewer and fewer people want to live there.

This is especially true in older neighborhoods, which sometimes struggle because parents are wary of living in a place with small yards, busy streets, troubled schools, or few other kids. This makes it doubly important that households without kids feel at home in the community. Many childless couples or singles are devoted to their pets and, just like parents, may reluctantly pull up stakes and move to a newer suburban house because they feel it's best for Rover or Puff, who can roam a big lawn away from busy streets.

The first step to making a place pet-friendly is to tame the traffic passing through your area. Traffic calming — an increasingly popular set of street improvements, ranging from narrower traffic lanes to more visible crosswalks to speed bumps, which get drivers to slow down — is the best way to keep dogs and cats (and everyone) safe.

For most dogs, the number one priority in life is a place where they can run, jump, and play off-leash with other dogs. Many forward-looking towns from Athens, Georgia, to Cedar Rapids, Iowa, to Moscow, Idaho, have set aside space for special "dog parks," which are usually fenced-off areas of city parks. Edmonton, Alberta, has eight of them. Prospect Park in Brooklyn even has a dog beach, where pooches can take a dip in the evening and early morning hours. These dog parks often become a lively hub of activity for two-legged neighbors, too.

The truth is that nothing brings people together better than dogs. They provide the perfect excuse to spark a conversation with a total stranger. "Is that a Bernese Mountain Dog?" or "How old is your puppy?" Anywhere people are out walking their dogs will be a place with a good sense of community.

RESOURCES

Dog parks:
www.ecoanimal.com/dogfun/
www.dogpark.com

Sing Along

Community choirs create social harmony

In Victoria, British Columbia, more than 250 people have joined the Gettin' Higher Choir, a proudly amateur outfit that welcomes everyone, no matter how limited their musical abilities. "We shouldn't leave something as important as music to the professionals," says choir director Shivon Robinsong. The Gettin' Higher Choir has no auditions and no rejections. Everyone is welcome.

Robinsong, who once viewed herself as the only untalented member of a very musical family, points out that in traditional societies, no one is excluded from singing. "Your voice is simply your voice," she tells choir members, "like your nose is your nose. It's nothing to worry over."

Music and dance are strong magnets for community interaction. These young performers drew an enthusiastic audience at Crossroads Mall in Bellevue, Washington.

The choir, which recently celebrated its tenth anniversary, puts on regular public concerts with the proceeds going to charitable causes, such as Power of Hope, an arts-based workshop for teens, or a program that assists a poor village in Mozambique.

You'll find similar community choirs popping up all across the continent, from the Syracuse Community Choir in upstate New York to the Eugene Peace Chorus in Oregon.

Val Rogers, director of the Eugene Peace Chorus, told writer Carol Estes of *Yes!* magazine, "These choirs are creating a new paradigm for choral singing. We're motivated by much more than aesthetics alone. We're singing for … a better society, to reinforce values that are vital to us, and to reclaim some of our cultural commons."

RESOURCES

Shivon Robinsong's community choir leadership training: www.shivon.com

Yes! magazine article on community choirs: www.yesmagazine.org

Organize Your Block

It's the best defense against crime, but also an opportunity to make your street come alive

In place after place, block clubs have shown themselves to be one of the most effective strategies to thwart crime. The number of burglaries, assaults, and other problems, large and small, drops significantly when neighbors look out for each other. Criminals go elsewhere to do their dirty work.

But why stop there? Once you've organized the neighbors to fight crime, why not tackle other inspiring goals? Judy Robinson of Sacramento wrote to *Making Places*, the on-line magazine of Project for Public Spaces, about all the fun she has with people on her block. **"I am blessed to live in such a perfect neighborhood,"** she said about East **Sacramento.** "We interact and we look after each other. We're a village."

Besides the typical but important neighborly acts, like taking in the mail or looking after pets and plants when others go on vacation, Robinson and her neighbors have initiated a whole round of seasonal festivities.

- At Halloween, several people on the block transform their homes into haunted houses for the delight of trick-or-treaters.
- One particularly artistic neighbor decorates the street-lamps for different seasons throughout the year.
- At Christmas time, many residents set aside a night to go caroling around the neighborhood and then come back inside to enjoy the warmth of cocoa and a sampling of holiday sweets from kitchens up and down the block. Everyone takes home a plateful of their favorite treats.
- In the spring, folks swap cuttings from their gardens; at harvest time, they share the bounty of backyard vegetable patches.

Along N Street in nearby Davis, California people have come together to create a Common House where everyone on the block can gather for meals, activities, or just to watch the big game on TV.

It's part of the broader vision of N Street residents to become a cohousing community. Cohousing, a modern equivalent of the traditional village where everyone looks out for one another, was invented in Denmark and is now a common housing option in Scandinavia, the Netherlands, and Germany. It is also beginning to take root in the United States, with 200 communities in more than 30 states.

Cohousing updates the '60s ideal of communal living to include a combination of private and community spaces. Households generally have their own residences, kitchens, and yards, but also enjoy the common house, where community meals and events take place. Other shared facilities can include gardens, fields, workshops, kids' playrooms, libraries, volleyball courts, and so forth.

Most cohousing communities are new constructions. But N Street is one example of an existing block deciding to become a more closely connected community. It began when two neighbors tore down their backyard fence in 1986 and now includes 17 households. The common house was purchased and remodeled in 1991 and features a community kitchen, dining room, and rec room with a piano, TV, and foosball table.

RESOURCES

Cohousing Association of the
    United States:
    www.cohousing.org
N Street Cohousing:
    www.nstreetcohousing.org

Neighbors mark Halloween and the Latin American Day of the Dead with a spooky parade in Toronto's Dufferin Grove neighborhood.

© Laura Berman/GreenFuse Images

Get Your Daily Dose of Vitamin T

Tribalism cures loneliness and alienation. Here are questions to help you see if you are getting enough

Do you miss the days when everything seemed more spirited and spontaneous? Instead of having to phone or e-mail friends to arrange time together three weeks from now (and often feeling in the mood to do something else when that time finally comes), you knew you'd run into them soon — probably that same day, since you all lived in the same area and frequented the same hangouts. Life was wondrously impromptu then and seemed somehow richer and certainly easier.

Nicholas Albery knew how you feel. "In my middle-age isolation," he wrote on his website in 2000, "I truly miss the convivial tradition of just dropping in on a neighbor for a conversation and a cup of coffee." Albery, an English author and social visionary, who died in a car wreck in 2001, was a pioneer in using the Internet to build community. But he was also keenly aware of how modern conveniences like the Internet, jet airplanes, cars, and mobile phones divorce us from our local world. New technologies enable us to expand our horizons by hooking up with far-flung people who share our exact same interests, yet it can still feel like something's missing.

That's only natural, Albery wrote, because "for most of human history we lived in small tribal groups of 50 to 250 people, and at an instinctual level we still crave bonds to people outside our immediate families. It's psy-chologically nourishing to feel connected to those we live among, not necessarily as close friends but as acquaintances with whom we can enjoy a regular chat …. We have a built-in, probably biologically rooted, need to live in proximity with a tribe, working and celebrating cooperatively within a geographical neighborhood."

Recognizing the lack of informal connections in his life, Albery advocated reintroducing a tribal bond to neighborhood life as the cure. Vitamin T, he called it. He organized a tea party for his block in northwest London, which has turned into an annual affair. "Even this token event," he noted with pleasure, "is beginning to boost our sense of community and increase our inclination to help each other out."

Further exploring the idea of tribalism as a cure for the isolation of modern life, he and a few friends came up with the following list of questions you can use to monitor the health of your own community.

Here are questions to help you see if you need more vitamin T. (By "local people" he means folks living in your part of town who you are likely to cross paths with on a regular basis, but who are not family members.)

1. Roughly how many local people (neighbors, store clerks, people at the bus stop, etc.) have you chatted with in the last week?

2. Roughly how many familiar people have you said "hi" or nodded to in passing on the street or in a public place during the last week?

3. How many times did you engage in a tribal ritual — for example, a religious service, a meal with neighbors, a drink with others at the local coffee shop or tavern, etc. — in your neighborhood last week?

4. If you were seriously ill, how many people could you count on to visit you or help with meals and other tasks?

5. How many people in the neighborhood would you feel comfortable dropping in on for a conversation without a prior invitation?

6. How many local people do you know with whom you'd feel comfortable discussing personal matters and worries?

7. How many local people understand your own goals and aspirations in life and support you in trying to achieve them?

8. To what extent do you feel that you are part of a connected and caring local community?

RESOURCES

Nicholas Albery's legacy: www.globalideasbank.org (This is an Internet compendium of social inventions — great ideas to improve society — gathered by Albery and colleagues, including many submissions from people around the world.)

The World's Greatest Ideas edited by Nicholas Albery and others (New Society Publishers, 2001).

These toddlers in Boston insist their parents take them to the Public Gardens every day so they can meet up with their pals.

Chapter 2

Where Everybody Knows Your Name

How to create great places to hang out

 Stop, look, and listen

 Enjoy more time out in public

 Make the most of what you've got

 Rediscover the front yard

 Offer people a place to sit

 Tear down fences

 Think small for big results

A family in Riverside, California, takes maximum advantage of a popular public space.

Stop, Look, and Listen

The best way to improve a place is to pay close attention to how people use it

It happens all too often. You find yourself in a plaza, park, or business district that has undergone a fancy, highly touted redevelopment — and no one's there. It's sad to see how gobs of money and people's high hopes can go into something that doesn't work out. And it's usually easy to see why it doesn't work. It wasn't designed with the people who would use it in mind. A project can look great on paper and even very impressive in real life when it's completed. It can win all sorts of architecture and planning awards and still not succeed at its basic mission: creating a place where people want to go.

"What were they thinking?" is probably your first reaction to such a place. "They really botched the job!" But flawed thinking is usually not the problem. It goes deeper than that. The real failure was not spending enough time looking at the place and listening to the people who go there. The most brilliantly conceived ideas don't mean much if planners, designers, developers, and even citizens don't do their homework by noticing how people really use a particular place.

In many years of studying how places work in communities all over the world, we at

PPS are constantly surprised by what we see. Take something as simple as a trash can. What could be more straightforward? Well, we often see folks using them for seating. Right away, that tells us that benches are needed in the new plan for that place. We've seen inventive people use trash cans as a desk for writing out checks to pay household bills or as a stove to cook clams.

It's remarkable what you discover when you take time to pay attention. Or as that great American philosopher Yogi Berra once put it, "You can see a lot just by observing."

New York's Bryant Park is a lovely green expanse behind the public library at 42nd Street and 6th Avenue. On paper, Bryant Park should be a great asset to the city, an oasis of grass and trees amid the skyscrapers of midtown Manhattan. But in the 1980s, few people went there except drug dealers and homeless people. PPS was invited to help with a redevelopment plan for Bryant Park. We spent a lot of time hanging out there, watching what went on and talking to people about what they thought of the place. Our staff interviewed the drug dealers and homeless people to find out what attracted them to the park.

We found that what drug dealers and homeless people liked about Bryant Park was exactly what most other people didn't like. The park entrances were narrow, and it was not easy to know what was happening inside the park. Indeed, not much was happening, which was why homeless people found it a good place for sleeping. PPS's recommendations to widen the entrance, remove shrubbery that blocked views into the park, and add some stands selling refreshments were implemented as part of a makeover, and now Bryant Park is one of the most well-loved (and well-used) spots in New York.

The same thing can work in your neighborhood. Just spend time in a place that you think could become more of an asset for the community. Hang out there at different times of day, on different days of the week, and in every season and all kinds of weather. Watch what goes on and talk to people who are there. Make a map of how the place is used. Then you'll have a clear picture of what can be done to improve the place.

RESOURCE

How to Turn a Place Around (Project for Public Spaces, 2000). Pages 51 to 53 are particularly relevant.

Make the Most of What You've Got

Public spaces are more than the sum of their parts. Little things can add up to a great place

Take a humble spot in your neighborhood — a bus stop or a branch library — and consider how you could gradually fashion it into a hub of public activity. Add a bench to the bus stop, then a trash receptacle and a drinking fountain, and it changes the whole feel of the corner. A regular Saturday-morning story time, along with a community message board out front and a playground for tots, transforms the library into a community center. Then see what happens at either location when a coffee shop with sidewalk tables opens, some public art is created, and vendors arrive selling ice cream or garden produce. *Voilà!* You've got a great hangout, a place you'll visit even when you're not taking the bus or looking for a book. You show up because you know something will be happening there.

This phenomenon is known as triangulation. This simply refers to the way elements in a public place build on one another, creating something more than the sum of its parts. It's synergy. At PPS, we call it the Power of Ten, meaning that if there are at least ten things you can do in a particular spot, it will likely become a popular destination for people in the neighborhood. This is the principle behind the world's favorite places. St. Mark's Square in Venice is really just a public square near the water with a church, coffee shops, and lots of pigeons. Yet the way these things work together make it one of the most romantic destinations on earth.

You could create a version of *Piazza San Marco* in your own community. Maybe tourist guidebooks will never write it up, but you will be able to enjoy it each day. Take a vacant lot and turn it into a junior version of the Boston Common, as a neighborhood group did on Dudley Street in Boston's Roxbury district. The Portland, Oregon-based group City Repair Project advocates that every neighborhood have its own public square. City Repair specializes in turning intersections into public gathering places, such as the big red labyrinth painted at the corner of Southeast 19th and Washington, with a herb garden and public benches nearby. Or the shrine to La Virgen de Guadalupe at Southeast 8th and Ankeny, on a corner where Mexican day laborers wait to be picked up for jobs. City Repair's ideas are now being embraced by groups in Seattle and Olympia, Washington; State College, Pennsylvania; and Asheville, North Carolina.

If it works on Chapel Street, a place folks avoided in New Haven, it can work anywhere. Once a thriving business district, Chapel Street was devastated by the urban decline that hit New Haven, Connecticut, particularly hard. By the early 1980s, only 5 percent of the area's residential and commercial spaces were occupied.

Almost everyone had given up on the place.

But not Joel Schiavone, a savvy and stubborn developer who saw potential where others saw only blight. Schiavone took a close look at the small things that, taken together, could transform the neighborhood. Indeed, he says it was always his goal to turn the area around without making it look any different. He convinced city officials to undo the damage of an earlier street-widening project by expanding the sidewalks so that Chapel Street felt like a place you'd want to hang out. Soon, a café expanded with outdoor seating, two more cafés opened, and a newspaper vendor set up shop. There are now nightclubs, restaurants, several theaters, and shops selling everything from bicycles to jewelry.

"The whole thing is like a mosaic," Schiavone explains. "Each piece needs to be carefully considered: street furniture, flowerboxes, a particular tenant for a storefront, tree plantings. If it's done right, all these things come together to create a real neighborhood."

RESOURCES

City Repair Project:
  www.cityrepair.org

City Repair's Placemaking Guidebook (City Repair Project, 2003)

Chapel Street: "Chapel Street," www.pps.org/gps

Almost given up for dead in the 1980s, Chapel Street in New Haven, Connecticut, sprang back to life thanks to modest improvements like trees, trash receptacles, and a wider sidewalk.

Offer People a Place to Sit

Any gathering spot will become more lively if folks have a comfortable spot to relax

A key ingredient of lively, safe, fun neighborhoods is public spaces where people will spontaneously gather. People out on the streets bring a community magically alive. You get to know your neighbors, you feel secure, and you have a place to hang out.

And there's one simple way to do this: give everyone a spot where they can sit down. A bench or chairs can transform a lonely space into a lively place.

People out walking or out shopping will stop to rest their legs. Others will then sit down, and conversations will arise. Soon people will make a point of heading there, knowing they'll find company.

That's the basic principle behind the charming squares in Latin American or European cities. You can spend a pleasurable afternoon just sitting in Rome's Piazza Navona or Prague's Old Town Square or Mexico City's Plaza Hildago, soaking up all the life happening around you. Think how much more fun this would be in your own community, where the intriguing people passing by are your neighbors.

The same principle is at work in the town commons of New England, the courthouse squares in small towns throughout the South and Midwest, and the bustling outdoor shopping streets of many suburbs such as Santa Monica, California, or Oak Park, Illinois.

This principle also holds true in the largest and busiest cities of the world. One of the first jobs Project for Public Spaces worked on was at

People everywhere are looking for a comfortable place to watch the world pass.

Rockefeller Center, the huge complex conceived in the 1930s as the town square for Manhattan. Today this is one of New York's most beloved spots, even though it is technically a private space. It's a favorite place where shoppers can rest in between Fifth Avenue stores, where office workers can nibble a snack, and where out-of-town visitors can catch their breath amid all the hustle and bustle.

But 30 years ago, the Center's managers weren't quite sure if they wanted the public hanging out there. They sought PPS's help to prevent people from sitting on ledges in the Channel Gardens, which leads to the famous skating rink. Specifically, they wanted to know what kind of spikes would work best to discourage would-be sitters.

Observing the area over a period of days, we concluded that people seeking a place to sit posed no problems at all and actually enhanced the experience of walking through the space. Instead of spikes, we suggested adding benches to the ledges of the Channel Gardens' planters, which could then be filled with flowers and decorations year-round. The managers followed our advice, and it changed the whole nature of the place. Now Rockefeller Center is full of people chatting and resting, resembling the town square it was meant to be.

RESOURCE

Rockefeller Center: "Channel
   Gardens," www.pps.org

More than a shopping mall

Lake Forest Park, Washington

One day a few years ago, Anne Stadler was in line to order lunch at the Town Center Mall in suburban Seattle when she overheard two men next to her lamenting the state of business. When she realized they were talking about her favorite part of the mall, Third Place Commons, she introduced herself. One of the men was a community-minded developer, Ron Sher, who had bought the failing shopping mall with the intention of turning it into a community gathering place. Sher, who had been inspired by *The Great Good Place,* a book by sociologist Ray Oldenburg that extols the benefits of meeting places outside the home and the workplace, had established a store in the mall, Third Place Books, which sat next to a large commons with a stage and cafés. The bookstore and the commons immediately became a haven for local families, who had a new reason to visit the once-dreary mall.

After this chance meeting, Stadler was struck by an idea: Why not have the community that

loves the Commons get involved in supporting and running it? She ran the idea by Sher, who agreed to donate the Commons area and stage to a new nonprofit that would fund and manage the space. Thus was born Friends of Third Place Commons, a public/ private partnership that includes the City of Lake Forest Park; the local arts council, library and community college; and a host of other nonprofit and educational community groups.

Today the Commons hosts a staggering variety of community events, including cooking lessons, club meetings, sports team parties, theatrical and musical perform-ances, and art exhibitions. It has become a much-loved gathering place for the whole community, from college students to families with young children to seniors.

RESOURCE

Third Place Commons:
   www.thirdplacebooks.com
   www.thirdplacecommons.org
The Great Good Place by Ray
   Oldenburg (Paragon House, 1989)

Once a failing shopping mall, Third Place Commons in Lake Forest Park, Washington, is now the pulsing heart of a suburban town.

SUCCESS STORY

Making paradise out of a parking spot

San Francisco, California

What's the best way to use a parking place? Conventional wisdom says "to park a car," but a group of activists known as Rebar has a different answer: to create much-needed public space. One afternoon in November 2005, Rebar fed the meter at a San Francisco parking spot and brought a new meaning to the word "park" by constructing a temporary green space complete with grass, a shade tree, and a bench. The project, dubbed "PARK(ing)," demonstrated how space for storing private vehicles, such as parking spots, can be altered to serve a more human purpose.

More than 70 percent of outdoor space in downtown San Francisco is dedicated to private vehicles, while only a small fraction is reserved for the public realm. Rebar chose the site for PARK(ing) by identifying an area that was underserved by public parks yet received plenty of sunshine. To install the temporary park, the activists "leased" a parking space and then unfurled 200 square feet of sod. Next they set down an old park bench and a 24-inch planter containing a tree. They posted a sign on the parking meter announcing that the grassy patch was open for public use, then began to receive visitors. The temporary park remained open from noon to 2 p.m.

Rebar sees PARK(ing) as a relatively simple exercise that other people could replicate in their own communities. It hopes the unusual sight of a parking spot transformed into a small public park will encourage people to question how public space is apportioned between cars and people. So far, groups in Trapani, Italy, and Santa Monica, California, have been inspired to install their own variations of PARK(ing). On September 21, 2006, Rebar staged the first PARK(ing) Day in San Francisco; more than a dozen local groups reclaimed parking spaces throughout the city in different ways.

RESOURCE

Rebar: www.rebargroup.org

Creative community activists in San Francisco turned a parking space into a temporary park, drawing attention to the fact that 70 percent of public space downtown is reserved for cars, not people.

Think Small for Big Results

Remarkable things happen when you plant a patch of petunias

Project for Public Spaces has distilled what it learned from its work in communities around the world into "11 Principles for Creating Great Community Places." Most of the advice centers on practical matters like "Have a vision," "The community is the expert," and "Form supports function," but one principle simply states, "Start with the petunias."

Petunias? What the heck do petunias have to do with the important business of making your neighborhood great? Well, actually quite a lot. Flowers can brighten up any place, whether it's the dowdy main street in a small town, a squalid vacant lot in an urban ghetto, or a dreary sidewalk near a suburban strip mall. And the presence of petunias or any other bloom reassures passersby that someone is committed to planting, watering, and weeding the flowerbed.

Civic groups in Shelburne Falls, a small town in Massachusetts, made the most of a bad situation by creating floral displays on a downtown bridge that had been abandoned when rail service shut down. That was in 1928, and the Bridge of Flowers has since become an attraction that draws attention and thousands of tourists to this out-of-the-way town.

But flowers do more than please the eye. They can lift a community's spirit and provide tangible proof that things are looking up. Planting flowers is a great way for a community to take that all-important first step.

"In creating or changing a public space, small improvements help to garner support along the way to the end result," writes PPS vice-president Kathy Madden in the book *How to Turn a Place Around.* "They indicate visible change and show that someone is in charge. Petunias, which are low cost and easy to plant, have an immediate visible impact. On the other hand, once planted, they must be watered and cared for. Therefore, these flowers give a clear message that someone must be looking after the place."

In New York, volunteers plant more than 3 million daffodils in parks each year. Originally conceived to commemorate September 11, the Daffodil Project now splashes color and raises spirits at more than 1,300 sites across the city, highlighting the potential for reclaiming neglected parks and other public spaces.

Harvard Business School professor John Kotter, who studies the dynamics of change, notes that people who succeed in improving things at a corporation, organization, or community "look for avenues that will produce some short-term wins, some visible changes that are associated with their effort, within six or 12 months. This gives them credibility and discourages the cynics .... Change of any magnitude tends to take time, so short-term wins are essential and must be an integral part of the long-term strategy."

Not all small actions leading to large results start with flowers. One exemplary project used white paint. Mulry Square was a dangerous intersection where three streets met in New York's Greenwich Village. Neighbors had long urged local officials to make the spot safer for pedestrians. Working with the New York City Department of Transportation and neighbors, PPS proposed an ambitious plan of traffic calming, tree plantings, and reconstructing the space to better serve people on foot. The city balked at making such big changes so rapidly, but it agreed to apply paint to create striped crosswalks between all the corners and to expand the space available to pedestrians. This demonstration project proved how well the proposed safety improvements worked, winning a commitment from the city to carry out the project.

"By experimenting with simple, visible, temporary actions like painting lines in the street, we were able to show the city how larger investments could pay off," explains Shirley Secunda, a member of the local community board.

RESOURCES

11 Principles for Creating Great Community Places: "11 Steps," www.pps.org

How to Turn a Place Around (Project for Public Spaces, 2000)

Shelburne Falls Bridge of Flowers: "Bridge of Flowers," www.pps.org

The Daffodil Project: www.ny4p.org

Mulry Square: "Mulry Square," www.pps.org

Kids intuitively understand what makes a great place, like these boys having a ball in Portland's Pioneer Square.

Enjoy More Time Out in Public

Wireless Internet and mobile phones offer new opportunities to indulge in café society

A hundred years ago, public spaces were central to everyone's lives. Jan Gehl, architecture professor at the Royal Danish Academy of Fine Arts in Copenhagen, explains how walking the streets and riding public transit were the only ways to get around town. Markets and shopping districts were the only places to purchase food and other necessities. Parks, taverns, churches, and the street itself were where people conducted their social lives, where they would meet with friends and neighbors.

But a chain of technological changes through the 20th century gave us less and less reason to leave our homes. Cars, telephones, radios, record players, refrigerators, televisions, air conditioners, VCRs, and computers transformed our daily lives to the point where many folks wonder if we need public places at all. But, as Kathy Madden of PPS notes, "The street, the square, the park, the market, the playground are the river of life. We are now rediscovering how essential they are to our well-being."

Citizens everywhere are clamoring for the chance to comfortably and conveniently gather in public. The last few years have seen an explosion in new or revitalized waterfronts, public markets, bike trails, parks, squares, shopping streets, libraries, and other places where people can mingle with one another. The new Campus Martius Park in Detroit is bringing life back downtown. Corpus Christi, Texas, created a bus transfer station that has become an unlikely social hub of the city. New coffee shops and sidewalk cafés are blossoming in towns and neighborhoods across the land.

It now appears that a new generation of technological breakthroughs can enhance, rather than diminish, our opportunities to participate in public life. Mobile phones,

Technological breakthroughs can enhance public life.

instant messaging, laptop computers, and wireless Internet make it possible to enjoy an afternoon in a café or park doing work that once confined us to office or home, notes Matt Blackett, a 33-year-old public-space advocate from Toronto. He explores these kinds of ideas in *Spacing*, a magazine devoted to public-space issues in Toronto.

You have the chance to be plugged into the world and your community at the same time. You can set up shop for a few hours at the library, a café, corner bar, or even a playground. Surf the Internet, catch up on your e-mail, and chat with friends or associates across the country while bumping into your neighbors and watching the interesting rhythms of daily life unfold. Who says you can't have the best of both worlds?

RESOURCES

Spacing magazine: www.spacing.ca

Jan Gehl: www.gehlarchitects.dk

Campus Martius: "Campus Martius," www.pps.org

Corpus Christi Staples Street Station: "Corpus Christi," www.pps.org

A playground for the whole town

Pass Christian, Mississippi

When both Hurricane Katrina and Hurricane Rita swept through Pass Christian, Mississippi (population 2,000), they leveled the town's War Memorial Park. The park's modest but popular playground became a rallying point for the community in its determination to recover from the disaster. Assisted by the national nonprofit KaBOOM! which helps communities build imaginative places for children to play, the people of Pass Christian made War Memorial Park a catalyst for the town's renewal.

The first step was to hold a "design day," where local children were asked to draw their dream playgrounds. For the next eight weeks, the community worked with KaBOOM!, corporate sponsor Home Depot, and other partners to produce a design for War Memorial Park based on the dream playgrounds. One particular project commemorated the hurricanes with a uniquely personal touch. Families donated their china, which had been destroyed by Katrina, and children used the broken pieces to create mosaic stepping stones.

The park's rebirth culminated on "build day," when volunteers constructed the entire playground in one day. All told, 550 volunteers from Pass Christian and neighboring towns came together to help in the planning and construction. "The process helped unite the community and neighboring communities," says KaBOOM!'s Sarah Pinsky. "Before the storm, communities were so independent, but now they are helping each other, sharing resources, and supporting each other's efforts in rebuilding."

Today, War Memorial Park is a real community place. Local businesses have located right next to the park. At lunch, all the benches are full. All community events are now held there. And children, families, and people from different walks of life use the playground at all times.

RESOURCE

KaBOOM! www.kaboom.org

Although devastated by Hurricane Katrina, people in Pass Christian, Mississippi, didn't give up on their town. They pooled their talents to rebuild a local park according to plans mapped out by local kids.

SUCCESS STORY

Brock McNally

How skateboarders saved a park

Tacoma, Washington

Until recently, city officials in Tacoma, Washington, cracked down on skateboarding in parks by installing skate-prevention devices (commonly called Skate-Stoppers, the name of a leading brand), often with disastrous results. Illicit activity increased in Thea's Park on the waterfront after the city put Skate-Stoppers at a popular skateboarding spot there. Without the skateboarders, fewer people used the park, and graffiti, broken glass, and drug-dealing all increased. In 2005, Peter Whitley, Brock McNally, and Matthew Levens — a group of skateboarding advocates — approached the parks department with a commonsense solution: Revive the park by reintroducing skateboarding. City officials were ready to listen because they recognized the park was in a downward spiral. Working together, the advocates and the city removed the Skate-Stoppers and established a regular inspection and cleanup routine.

This success story represents a big departure from strategies that have prevailed since the 1970s, when skateboarding in public spaces was first looked upon as an act of vandalism. "Now that skaters are interacting with each other and rebuilding communities disrupted by a lack of gathering places," says Whitley, "many are seeing that it's possible to address the 'public image' damage done during the '80s by creating skateboarding spaces that allow for non-skateboarding uses simultaneously."

Today, Thea's Park is clean and used for many different activities, including kite-flying, picnics, dog-walking, and kayak launches. It benefits from the presence of skateboarders, who look out for the park and are appreciated by other park users. Tacoma is now looking at designing another mixed-use space that would allow skate-boarding, but not to the exclusion of other activities. In any community, collaboration between the skateboarding community, park planners, and city officials can create popular public spaces that generate youthful energy.

RESOURCES

Tacoma Skateparks:
tacomaskateparks.org

Skaters for Public Skateparks:
www.skatersforpublic
skateparks.org

Skateboard enthusiasts in Tacoma, Washington, proved to local authorities that their presence in a waterfront park actually reduced crime and encouraged non-skaters to visit. That's when the "no skating" signs came down.

A man relishes the social benefits of his front yard.

Rediscover the Front Yard

Rather than hiding out back, greet the world from your porch or stoop

We usually think of public space as places where everyone goes, like a park or a business district. But Danish architecture professor Jan Gehl, who for the past 40 years has been researching how people use cities, notes there are several distinct kinds of public spaces.

- Parks, downtowns, the library, or a farmers market qualify as fully public spaces. Anyone is free to go there and do what they wish (within reason).

- Front yards and residential sidewalks, on the other hand, are semi-public spaces. You are permitted to be there, but only for short periods and specific purposes. Such places often serve as informal gathering spots, but you could not just sit down to play music or read a book the way you might in a park.

- A flower patch, porch, or stoop at the front of a residence is a semi-private place. A stranger can appreciate it and even call out hello to a resident, but it's not acceptable to actually enter the space unless invited.

- A backyard is generally thought of as private space, the same as the house itself.

Some historians have noted that the gradual shift of outdoor life at home from the front porch to the back patio is a key element in our declining sense of community. Indeed, after World War II, front porches disappeared from houses alto-gether. They were replaced in many new communities by the dull, blank wall of garage doors.

Thankfully, front porches are back in fashion today as a distinguishing architectural fea-ture on many new houses. But more than a status symbol, a front porch is a great place to hang out. You can greet your neighbors, make new acquain-tances, and keep an eye on what's going on down the block. It's a wonderful spot to eat meals in the warmer months and set up a reading lamp and comfy chairs to catch the cool evening breezes.

There are certainly times when we might prefer the pri-vacy of the backyard, but too often going there becomes a reflexive habit when we'd really prefer to be part of what's hap-pening in the world around us.

Sitting on the stoop is a great city pastime that has become endangered as new buildings dispense with front stoops altogether or make them so small as to be useless. If you are lucky enough to have one, celebrate it as a place to read the newspaper, drink a beer, gaze at the stars, or sit down next to a neighbor to view the passing parade of life.

In Minneapolis, among other places, the front yard is regaining its rightful position as a center of community activity. A few years ago, an arts organization went to work building handsome Adirondack chairs, painting them bright green and giving them to people who promised to lounge in them in the front yard. The Open Eye Figure Theatre, which works pri-marily with puppets, launched a summer neighborhood tour in which local families offered their front yards for performances and invited all the kids in the neighborhood.

Jean Johnson and Niel Ritchie built a beautiful second-story deck looking over their backyard in Minneapolis's East Harriet neighborhood. It was a wonderful place to relax, but they often felt cut off from the life of the neighborhood. So they constructed a front yard patio, complete with wooden lawn fur-niture and a fire pit, that soon became the scene of frequent parties and countless impromptu conversations. "It changed our lives in big ways," Johnson says. "We felt much better plugged in to everything that was happening."

They have since downsized to a smaller house — with a great front porch, Johnson notes — and another family is spending its summer, and even spring and autumn, evenings out in the front yard.

RESOURCES

Jan Gehl: *Life Between Buildings: Using Public Space* (Danish Architectural Press, 2001)

Open Eye Figure Theatre: www.openeyetheatre.org

Tear Down the Fences

Sharing backyard space creates a comfy neighborhood commons

In many neighborhoods, back-yards once served as something of a town green where kids could toss Frisbees, play tag, and run back and forth between each other's houses. The area closest to each home still retained a private feel, but the clotheslines often marked the end of strictly private property and the start of a semi-public zone. You still see this in some small towns, but in most bigger communities the neighborhood commons has been enclosed.

Around Seattle, architect Ross Chaplin is helping revive the custom of a town green with the popular cottage communities he designs. At the Greenwood Avenue Cottages in Shoreline, Washington, eight houses with small fenced yards open onto a shared commons with flowers, fruit trees, a lawn, and a community building with a workshop and party room.

People in the Federal Hill neighborhood of inner-city Baltimore created cozy back-yard greens by tearing down the fences. Residents of 11 row houses came together to create Chandlers Yard, a tree-shaded courtyard where residents now relax with coffee and the morning paper or sit down for a chat with the neighbors. It features a landscaped path and a flagstone terrace with a patio table. The commons has caused a significant leap in property values on the block, but most Chandlers Yard residents don't care — they aren't moving anywhere.

In the Washington Street neighborhood of Boulder, Colorado, Vivian and Dominique Getliffe decided to plant a garden together with their next-door neighbors. It became a catalyst to bring the whole block together. Eight families now share the garden and a common yard. Big potluck picnic dinners, planned and unplanned, are now a regular occurrence on Washington Street. "Private yards with fences allow us to push the world away," resident Dan Diehl told the authors of *Superbia!* a book about improving suburban living. "But the more you push it away, the lonelier you are."

If you're interested in creating your own backyard Eden, you'll find a wealth of information and inspiration at the website of Community Greens, a joint project of the National Trust for Historic Preservation and Ashoka, an organization promoting social innovation. The Community Greens site is packed with details and photos of successful projects. "When they are well-designed and well-managed, community greens have remarkable benefits," the site declares. Such backyard greens can provide:

- Accessible and safe play areas for kids.

- A heightened sense of community as neighbors are drawn together to create, manage, protect, and enjoy their backyard commons.

- A relaxing spot to hang out, either by yourself or with neighbors.
- Increased safety and security because neighbors can look after each other more effectively than they can with privacy fences blocking the view.
- Improved stability because people on blocks with community greens move less often and are more likely to invest in improvements to their own house and yard.
- Environmental improvements as people cooperate to plant gardens and trees, which in turn reduce stormwater runoff and provide habitat for birds and other small animals.

- An attractive alternative to sprawl by making living in cities and built-up suburbs more attractive, especially to families with children.

RESOURCES

Ross Chapin Architects: www.rosschapin.com

Community Greens: www.communitygreens.org (Includes the story on Chandler's Yard and other projects)

Superbia! 31 Ways to Create Sustainable Neighborhoods by Dan Chiras and Dave Wann (New Society Publishers, 2003)

Young people in Amsterdam greet the world with a splashy party rather than a forbidding fence.

Chapter 3

Going Places

How to tame traffic and improve transportation

 Imagine your neighborhood with 50 percent less traffic

 Calm the traffic

 Cut down on your driving

 Help drivers learn to share the road

 Use street smarts to rethink traffic safety

 Seize new opportunities for bikes and pedestrians

 Learn from abroad

Imagine Your Neighborhood with 50 Percent Less Traffic

Visionary activist David Engwicht says creativity is our most important tool for rebuilding communities

So what would your neighborhood look like if the needs of people mattered more than the needs of automobiles? One of the most interesting thinkers playing with this question is David Engwicht, a former seminary student and window washer who began looking at transportation in bold new ways after hearing about plans to widen a road near his home in a suburb of Brisbane, Australia. He attended a public meeting inclined to think widening was a good idea, but changed his mind after hearing neighbors' stories about how faster traffic on the street would disrupt their lives. Engwicht wrote a pamphlet and

later a book *Reclaiming Our Cities and Towns* in which he outlined his thoughts and suddenly found himself an international spokesman for the idea of traffic calming — a new invention to tame reckless and thoughtless motorists by making physical changes to streets (e.g., narrow lanes, speed bumps, etc.) that force people to drive slower and pay more attention to pedestrians.

Engwicht's ultimate goal is to reduce the volume of traffic in cities by as much as 50 percent, as well as reducing cars' speed. And he proposes some extraordinary means to achieve this, including waving to

Australian pedestrian advocate David Engwicht sets up a throne in the middle of busy streets all over the world to show that cars are not king of the road. He can be seen here in the Champs-Élysées (left) and Times Square (right).

motorists, putting a bench in front of your home, adding antlers to your bicycle helmet, dressing your kids as dragons … anything to break down the barriers between drivers sealed inside their autos and everyone else. For his part, Engwicht is investing thousands of dollars to outfit his own front yard with a neighborhood bread oven and a large sculpture shaped like a mushroom that splashes water into a pond. If that doesn't get drivers to slow down and take a closer look, Engwicht says he doesn't know what will.

"We have this strange fixation that fast movement always equals progress," he states, "and going slow is stagnation. But I think we are all wanting a little better balance between our need to move and our need to feel comfortable and at home where we live. Speed disconnects us from our surroundings. It can be a loss as well as a gain."

Engwicht weaves a vision of the future every bit as compelling as the dream of personal mobility represented by the car. He prophesies that in 30 years people will still use cars, but most of us will likely be members of co-ops in which several households share one vehicle. Traffic will be much lighter, and people will walk and bike far more than they do today. Cafés, grocery stores, bakeries, shops, and small parks will pop up in the middle of what today are residential streets. People will still travel for fun, but they will spend more time exploring their own towns and neighborhoods.

"We'll just amble down the streets in no hurry," he envisions. "The front yards will become the center of social life as people just hang out and enjoy each other's company, with plenty of time to relax, reflect, and play. If you're going somewhere by car you'll feel that you're missing out on so much. "

Engwicht counsels everyone to use their sense of playfulness and dreams as guides to creating the kind of neighborhood they want. No idea is too outlandish if it can inspire people to make changes.

RESOURCES

David Engwicht: www.lesstraffic.com

Reclaiming Our Cities and Towns by David Engwicht (New Society Publishers, 1993)

Street Reclaiming by David Engwicht (New Society Publishers, 1999)

Mental Speed Bumps by David Engwicht (Envirobooks, 2005, www.mentalspeedbumps.com)

And here are other people trying out Engwicht's ideas in Vancouver, Washington (top) and and Missoula, Montana (bottom).

DAVID ENGWICHT

DAVID ENGWICHT

Calm the Traffic

You'll be shocked at the changes in your community after you take back the streets from exclusive use by autos

Research shows that striking visual elements, like these huge bunnies in Midland, Michigan, will cause cars to slow down.

Speeding traffic is probably the single biggest problem that besets North American neighborhoods. Busy streets with rushing vehicles spark a vicious cycle in which people who might prefer to walk or bike end up driving because they fear for their safety. Numerous studies have shown that the speed of traffic, much more than the volume, is what poses a threat to pedestrians. One study conducted by the British government found that 85 percent of pedestrians hit by cars traveling 40 miles an hour (not an uncommon speed on streets in many American communities) were killed. In comparison, only 5 percent of pedestrians hit by vehicles traveling 20 miles an hour were killed.

Children are probably the biggest losers in this system, since they can no longer wander and play in the streets and must stay inside when they're not supervised by an adult. (According to the organization Transportation Alternatives, being hit by a car is one of the leading causes of death for children aged 5 to 14 in New York City.) For thousands of years, city streets were a place to socialize as well as a pathway for all forms of transportation. But over the past century, they have been taken over for the exclusive use of automobiles.

Lowering speed limits is one logical response to this problem. But many people herald traffic calming as a more effective way of keeping drivers from roaring down their streets because it's enforced 24 hours a day, not just when a police car is on the scene. Traffic calming has the potential to transform your neighborhood as it has many others around the world.

Traffic calming encompasses a whole set of common sense street designs that can help you increase safety and satisfaction for folks in your neighborhood. The aim is twofold: to slow the speed of traffic and to give drivers a visual reminder that they must share the street with people on foot, on bicycles, in wheelchairs, and in baby strollers. Speed bumps, narrowed streets, stop signs, brightly painted crosswalks, on-street parking, median strips down the middle of streets, bans on right turns at red lights, crosswalks raised a few inches

above the roadway, and curbs that extend into intersections all help make the streets safer and more pleasant for pedestrians.

Opponents claim that traffic calming simply shoves traffic onto someone else's street. But numerous studies have shown that traffic calming not only reduces speeds but can actually decrease traffic in general as people make fewer trips in their car, either by running a number of errands on one outing or by switching to biking, walking, or taking public transit. When Greenwich Village's Washington Square Park was closed to cars in the early 1960s, transportation engineers' studies showed that traffic on nearby streets decreased — exactly the opposite of what opponents of the plan had warned. Transportation officials in Nuremberg, Germany, documented the same phenomenon many years later when they closed a major downtown street.

Another complaint is that narrower streets, frequently a traffic-calming goal, are more dangerous for motorists. But when the city of Longmont, Colorado — a booming Denver suburb — examined the 20,000 accidents on local streets over an eight-year period, it found that "as street width widens, accidents per mile per year increase exponentially."

Towns everywhere are restoring sanity and serenity to their streets. Eugene, Oregon, which used to require that all streets be at least 28 feet wide, now allows some to be as narrow as 20 feet. Wellesley, Massachusetts, faced with a plan to widen its congested main street, instead chose to narrow it and expand the sidewalks to encourage walking. Even in auto-happy southern California, the cities of San Bernardino, Riverside, and Beverly Hills have narrowed major commercial streets. Meanwhile, in San Mateo County, just south of San Francisco, communities along the famous El Camino Real Highway are working to revive their downtowns by implementing traffic calming and creating better public spaces for people.

Traffic calming is much more than just a way to promote safer streets. Australian town planner Phil Day explains that it "involves a fundamental rethinking of metropolitan planning and organization — and a revised emphasis on quality rather than quantity of life. Some may see the ultimate goal as the calming of society itself."

RESOURCES

Traffic calming: "Traffic calming," www.pps.org
Transportation Alternatives: www.transalt.org

Residents of Stonington, Connecticut, urge motorists to respect their neighborhoods.

Going to school on a walking bus

Toronto, Ontario, Canada

The Walking School Bus is an innovative new idea that parents and students in any town can copy on their own. Several children and at least one parent or caregiver walk to and from school together each day in a group that offers the safety of a ride in a bus or car with the chance for fresh air and exercise. Parents spend less time behind windshields and more on the sidewalks, so they better understand what can be done to make walking safer for their kids and everyone in the neighborhood. If people get in the habit of walking on their local streets every day, the thinking goes, they will start asking traffic engineers to design for pedestrian needs, not just cars.

First conceived by Australian David Engwicht in 1991, the idea has spread around the world. One of the leading advocates in North America is Toronto native Tom Samuels, who showed how to do it in his 1995 book *Safe Routes to School: The ABCs of Getting Your Kids There in One Piece.* In 1997, Samuels launched a national Safe Routes to School/Walking School Bus program as part of Health Canada's Active Living

Campaign. Later that year he relocated to Chicago, where he developed and implemented a Safe Routes to School/Walking School Bus program at 600 public schools involving more than 450,000 children.

Although the Walking School Bus has been effective in many places, Samuels stresses that it should be just the beginning of deeper changes. The real objective is to open people's minds to the need for safer, more walkable streets. It is not just about walking to school, but about getting everyone — from parents and children to transportation planners and engineers — to question the status quo of how our streets are designed.

RESOURCES

Walking School Buses:
   www.walkingschoolbus.org
Tom Samuels:
   www.americawalks.org
David Engwicht:
   www.lesstraffic.com
National Center for Safe Routes to Schools:
   www.saferoutesinfo.org

The walking school bus is a new twist on an old idea — a parent becomes the "driver" responsible for getting neighborhood kids to school safely.

Miracle on Main Street
Littleton, New Hampshire

Although it is home to just 6,000 residents, Littleton is the economic hub of New Hampshire's North Country. Concerned that its small-town character was in jeopardy from sprawl and traffic, the town applied for a grant from the federal Transportation and Community and System Preservation Pilot Program (TCSP).

The town adopted a unique process, asking everyone from students at the local high school to prominent businesspeople to identify the most important places along Littleton's Main Street and make suggestions on how to improve them. These folks then joined "neighborhood planning assemblies" that met in every conceivable venue — the opera house, the town diner, the seniors' center, the elementary school. Sometimes it seemed as though the entire town was involved.

The meetings inspired ideas that were previously unthinkable. Adults and young people, for example, shared their concerns about benches on Main Street. The town had removed most public seating years earlier, fed up by a few teenagers who would perch on benches and antagonize passersby. Young people pointed out that scarce seating meant "there's only enough space for the bad kids to sit down." Encouraging more young people to come downtown, rather than discouraging them in order to weed out a few troublemakers, was a far more effective solution to the problem.

Another issue was that the downtown's walkable core had shrunk because of suburban-style road design and business development. Littleton's Placemaking process resulted in a shared community vision to significantly expand downtown Littleton's walkable core without constructing new buildings. Simply adding a sidewalk between the bank and the ice-cream store, for instance, encouraged people to walk between the two. By providing crosswalks, wider sidewalks, better pedestrian amenities, and more gathering places, the town could renew its own sense of place. This helped connect Main Street's destinations and join them to the riverfront, resulting in a significant expansion of the area where local residents would routinely walk. By enlarging the area of downtown that is well served by sidewalks and pedestrian amenities, the perception of available parking increased without actually adding any new spaces, and a greater sense of community was instilled.

RESOURCE
Littleton, NH:
   www.pps.org/littleton

Everyone in Littleton, New Hampshire, had a chance to participate in meetings about how to keep the downtown healthy. As a community, they came up with a new vision of the American Dream, which was printed on T-shirts.

Cut Down on Your Driving

It's easier than you think — and will save a bundle of money

It's healthier for you and your community to leave the car at home, as this man visiting Kensington Market in Toronto has done.

The Union of Concerned Scientists has singled out the automobile as the biggest source of environmental problems in modern society. In the handbook *The Consumer's Guide to Effective Environmental Choices,* Michael Brower and Warren Leon note, "Alas, many of the things that cause the most damage are pretty fundamental to the American middle-class way of life. Nowhere is that fact more evident than in our reliance on the automobile."

Yes, we all know that traffic creates pollution, noise and a lack of community in many neighborhoods. For most Americans, however, life without a car is unimaginable. Still, according to the US census, a surprisingly high number of households get along without owning a car.

Car-Free Households

New York City	56 percent
Washington DC	37 percent
Philadelphia	36 percent
Boston	35 percent
Pittsburgh	30 percent
Chicago	29 percent
San Francisco	29 percent

Many of these people find that going without a car is easy. They get more exercise, feel healthier, know their neighbors better, and have money left over in the household budget for vacations, dinners out, special purchases, and savings. Folks who don't regularly drive also make a positive contribution to their community by putting one less car on the streets. If you live in an area with adequate public transit or good walking conditions, you might consider a car-free life. Even the occasional splurges on taxis or rental cars will seem a pittance compared to what you spend every month in auto payments, gas, repairs, licenses, and insurance.

Of course, 80 years of all-for-the-auto urban planning make it hard for some people to simply forsake cars, notably those who live or work in rural areas and outlying suburbs where sidewalks and public transit don't exist. Yet all of us could easily drive less. The average US household takes more than 12 separate automobile trips a day. You might be surprised how many of your travels could be done on bike, foot, or bus. Instead of driving to the gym to exercise, for instance, take up running, walking, or biking around the neighborhood. Save up your errands and do them on just one trip rather than a dozen. Or create your own transit service by coordinating travel with neighbors. All of these ideas will make you grateful you're spending less of your time behind the wheel.

Owning just one car is a strategy being adopted by more and more savvy families. It's easy to do if one adult in the family can figure out how to get to work or take care of other basic responsibilities each day by transit, car pool, bike, or foot. If an occasion arises when another vehicle is needed, there are always taxis, rental cars, and car-share programs, or maybe you can borrow a car from a neighbor. In addition to enjoying considerable financial savings and health benefits, one-car households find they get to know their hometowns better, seeing sights and meeting people they would miss if they were always hidden behind the windshield.

Car-sharing programs can reduce your dependence on autos while ensuring you have access to a car when you must pick up a sick child at school, need to cart some heavy item, or want to go out in the country on a Sunday afternoon. They are ideally suited for car-free families or those with just one vehicle. In Stockholm, Sweden, for instance, only 20 percent of households own cars, but many belong to co-ops, where one vehicle is bought or leased by as many as a dozen families. In the Norwood/Quince neighborhood of Boulder, Colorado, 40 people have joined a car-sharing club that rents cars by the hour.

Formal car-sharing programs and businesses are already well-established in Europe, where they began 20 years ago in Switzerland and Germany. There are now 17 car-sharing programs in the United States, with 100,000 members in total. They are mostly in big cities but also in places as small as Fort Wayne, Indiana; Nevada City, California; and Rutledge, Missouri (population 103). Canada has 11 car-sharing programs, with 15,600 members sharing 779 vehicles.

RESOURCES

The Consumer's Guide to Effective Environmental Choices by Michael Brower & Warren Leon (Three Rivers Press, 1999)

Cutting Your Car Use by Randall Ghent with Anna Semlyen (New Society Publishers, 2006)

How to Live Well Without Owning a Car by Chris Balish (Ten Speed Press, 2006)

Divorce Your Car! Ending the Love Affair with the Automobile by Katie Alvord (New Society Publishers, 2000)

Car sharing: www.carsharing.net

Help Drivers Learn to Share the Road

With kind words and publicity campaigns, pedestrians stand up for their rights

For more than a century, escalating traffic volumes have been seen as an inevitable by-product of modern life. People might yearn for the calm and comfort of life before cars, but, until recently, few saw any hope of challenging the total dominance of cars in our society. Neighbors sadly and silently watched as the fabric of their communities was shredded to accommodate the ever-growing volume and speed of traffic.

But now, in town after town, citizens are speaking out, holding meetings, and fighting city hall (and in some cases working with city hall) on the issue of slowing down traffic. They are tired of worrying about the safety of their children, their pets, and their elderly and disabled friends, all of whom are imperiled by speeding drivers. They are determined to restore a sense of peace and community to their neighborhoods by reclaiming the streets from traffic. In Atlanta, for instance, pedestrian advocates sponsored a public event to mark the 50th anniversary of the death of *Gone with the Wind* author Margaret Mitchell, killed by a reckless taxi driver. In California, parents all over the state are busy mapping safe ways for kids to walk to school.

It begins with pedestrians and bicyclists speaking up. When motorists cut you off, say something. Yelling probably won't change their behavior (though it could make you feel better), but a calm reminder that people and bikes have a legal right to use the streets might make a difference. The last thing most drivers want is to endanger anyone. The problem is usually not with them, but with the fact that streets are designed with only autos in mind. Drivers have been conditioned to believe the road belongs to them. It's up to us to point out that they are legally obligated to share the road, and the best way to help them remember is with a smile. Let them know you're there, and make doubly sure to say thanks or offer a friendly wave when they show you some courtesy.

Pedestrian advocacy organizations are popping up in many places to promote better environments for walking. They lobby public officials for traffic calming and lower speed limits and conduct transportation studies to counter traffic engineers' claims that wider roads and more parking lots are beneficial to society.

"It's easy to become a pedestrian advocate," says **Ellen Vanderslice** of Portland, Oregon, whose harrowing attempts to cross a busy street with two toddlers turned her into an activist. "Find out who's making the decisions about traffic in your community," she advises, "and how the process works, and where you can make an impact. Find people who feel the same way and get a group together."

That's exactly what Vanderslice did, joining the

newly formed Willamette Pedestrian Coalition, which pressured the city for better walking conditions. Local officials didn't only listen; they also brought Vanderslice into city hall to devise a long-range plan to make Portland more pedestrian-friendly. When that project was completed, she became president of America Walks, a national coalition of pedestrian advocacy groups representing cities from Philadelphia to Honolulu.

RESOURCE

America Walks:
  www.americawalks.org

The true measure of neighborhood livability is whether senior citizens and disabled people can get around comfortably. If it's a good place for them, like this neighborhood in Paris, then it's good for everybody.

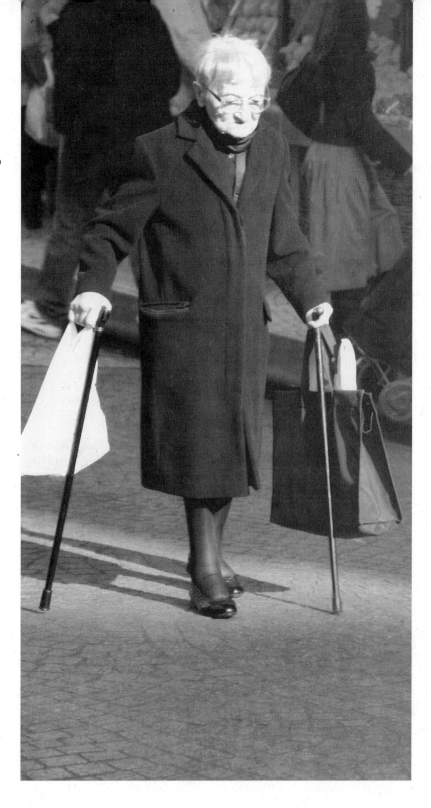

Use Street Smarts to Rethink Traffic Safety

Despite everything we've been told, stoplights on neighborhood streets often put pedestrians and motorists in peril

How many times has this happened to you? You're waiting at an intersection — on foot or in a car — and as you start to cross after the light turns green, a car almost clobbers you as it races through the red light.

Stoplights probably do more to encourage lawless and dangerous behavior than any invention since the pistol. Think about it. You see a stoplight in the distance when you're driving and naturally hurry up, usually exceeding the speed limit, so you don't have to stop. It's a human instinct, even among normally safe drivers who care about pedestrian safety.

A stop sign sends a much different message and works on drivers' instincts in an entirely different way. You know you must stop, so there's no incentive to speed. But you also know that soon you'll be able to move again. At a stoplight, in contrast, you may be stuck for more than a minute waiting for various turn arrows to run through their cycles. It's aggravating to sit still for so long, and you would do almost anything to avoid it — including driving recklessly fast and barreling through an intersection after the light has turned red.

Switching many stoplights to four-way stop signs will make the streets safer, quieter, and more pleasurable for both pedestrians and motorists. Yet, incredibly, many traffic engineers oppose this idea, claiming it's unsafe.

Kenneth Todd, an industrial engineer who has studied the subject in depth and published his findings in transportation journals, writes in the journal *Regulation,* "According to the Federal Highway Administration (FHWA) all-way stop intersections [usually 4-way stop signs] have the best safety record, with half as many accidents as those controlled by two-way stops or signals [stoplights]." Traffic engineers in Philadelphia confirmed this when they replaced 800 stoplights with four-way stops and saw pedestrian injuries decrease 49 percent.

Traffic engineers worry that drivers don't come to a full stop at stop signs, an argument Todd answers by noting, "Most drivers do not come to a full stop but treat the all-way stop as an all-way yield." However, that's no problem because "the yield sign has a safety record as good as the stop sign."

Indeed, stoplights actually contribute to congestion — accounting for "40 percent of vehicle delays," according to official reports quoted by Todd — not to mention stress, as drivers nervously scramble to make the light rather than comfortably settling into the safer and more relaxing rhythm of a street with stop signs.

The real reason some traffic engineers balk at more stop signs, Todd says, is because "FHWA's *Manual* has called the stop sign a device that causes considerable inconvenience to motorists."

For 80 years, traffic engineers have been trained to see

their job as moving cars through cities as rapidly as possible with a minimum of inconvenience. Little thought was given to how pedestrians, kids at play, and entire neighborhoods were inconvenienced and even terrorized by roaring traffic. You may still encounter this rigid thinking when you suggest installing stop signs or traffic calming to traffic planners or elected officials. The facts and figures they quote back to you are often slanted to back up their belief that anything that slows cars is, by definition, bad.

Forward-looking traffic engineers in forward-looking towns now recognize the importance of stop and yield signs. Coming off the Golden Gate Bridge into San Francisco, you'll stop at almost every corner on Marine Avenue, which ensures that the Marina district is not cut off from the bay by torrents of speeding traffic. In Madison, Wisconsin, many stoplights around town are set to flash red on and off during evening, nighttime, and some weekend hours, becoming yield signals that offer pedestrians and cross traffic a safe way to traverse busy arterial streets. This shows that stoplights in your town don't even need to be replaced, just reprogrammed. A flashing red light accompanying a stop sign is

The humble stop sign, reviled by many traffic engineers, is actually safer than stoplights in most cases.

another solution for intersections where city officials worry that motorists may not notice the sign alone.

There are big changes afoot among a new generation of traffic engineers who understand that moving cars is only part of the picture. What happens to communities themselves is also important. A new approach taking hold among transportation planning professionals is Context Sensitive Solutions, based on the insight that moving cars and trucks quickly and safely from one place to another is not the only point of transportation projects. It is equally important to link the places themselves and ensure that a road or other transportation facility enhances a place instead of degrading it. Central to this effort is concerted planning for pedestrians, bicyclists, and transit riders, who play a crucial role in ensuring roads work efficiently for a community. Many highway officials now recognize that most new and newly widened roads immediately fill up with cars because no one paid attention to other forms of transportation. State transportation departments and towns now focus on making the most of the roads they have, rather than constantly going back to widen them. Even the Federal Highway Administration is embracing these ideas and enlisted PPS to help it create a comprehensive website showing alternatives to the way America has built roads over the past 60 years.

RESOURCES

Kenneth Todd:
   kennethatodd@aol.com
Context Sensitive Design:
www.contextsensitivesolutions.org

Hot fun in the summertime

Paris, France

All too often, city halls and the public spaces around them are drab and forbidding places. (PPS recently named Boston's City Hall Plaza one of the worst public spaces in the galaxy, only half in jest.) This is not the case in Paris, where the plaza in front of the Hôtel de Ville (city hall) is always full of activity that changes with the seasons.

In the winter, for instance, the Hôtel de Ville hosts a skating rink that is open to the public. In the summer, the plaza becomes an extension of the famous Paris Plage (Paris Beach), an event that shuts down a segment of the city's riverside highway by converting it into a beach complete with sand, deck chairs, palm trees, and a multitude of games and activities. Beach umbrellas and lounge chairs are also set up in front of the Hôtel de Ville, where parents relax in the sun while children play in the sand. The event has been widely praised for giving low-income families access to open space and fun activities during the hot summer. At other times of year, the plaza is the scene of various festivals and celebrations, such as film screenings, food festivals, and expositions about the world's cultures.

The innovative steps Paris has taken to enliven its city hall offer ideas for all cities, large and small. One key lesson here is to stop acting out of fear. Many cities would be too worried about "the wrong sort" of people using the beach chairs to ever consider such a plan. Paris refused to be paralyzed by these concerns and, by coming up with a great idea, shows the possibilities inherent for all other cities — both large and small.

A beach resort appears in the center of Paris every summer when a major street along the Seine River is closed and filled with truckloads of sand.

Since 1991, the US federal government has provided money to towns wanting to promote walking, biking and transit. Although the sums are tiny compared to what highways get, it has triggered big improvements in many places, such as communities along the 47-mile Pinellas Bike Trail on the Gulf Coast of Florida.

Seize New Opportunities for Bikes and Pedestrians

After years of pushing all-for-the-auto policies, Washington is now serious about supporting alternative ways of getting around

Why are so many American communities bedeviled by noisy, ugly, polluting highways? And why do so few have first-rate rail transit? The answers are clear: For decades, the federal government would fund 90 percent of an interstate highway project and much less — or none — of a subway, light-rail, or commuter train line. That changed the face of America, as highways were slashed through the heart of vital communities, breaking their spirit and hastening the exodus of people to far-flung suburbs. In the same period, hardly any federal or state money went toward expanding rail lines and other alternatives

to the automobile. From the end of World War II to the opening of the Bay Area's BART transit system in 1972, only a few miles of subway lines were added nationally, compared to tens of thousands of miles of urban freeways and other highways. That gross imbalance has likely affected the growth and character of your own neighborhood.

The federal government of Canada, on the other hand, spent far less money on highway projects, and you can see the happy results today. Fewer freeways cut through the cores of Canadian cities (Vancouver has none at all in the city proper) and, as a result, the cities have seen less inner-city decline. Another significant factor in the relative vitality and attractiveness of Canadian cities compared to many struggling inner-city neighborhoods in the United States can be directly traced to government policies. Both nations rewarded veterans returning from World War II with generous support for buying homes. In the United

States, however, veterans were generally restricted to buying a new home, which helped spark the suburban boom of the 1950s. Canada sensibly offered vets financial support to buy any home, old or new, and that kept older districts of their cities appealing.

Thankfully, transportation policies in the United States have improved greatly thanks to legislation introduced by the late Senator Daniel Patrick Moynihan of New York and signed by former President George H.W. Bush. The 1991 Intermodal Surface Transportation Efficiency Act (ISTEA, pronounced "Ice-Tea") marked a major change in federal transportation policy. While providing billions to continue building and widening highways, ISTEA also set the precedent that communities could use a share of federal transportation dollars for transit, bicycle, pedestrian safety, and community enhancement projects.

This was just the opening that many communities had been waiting for, and America quickly bloomed with bike paths, walkways, light-rail lines, and transit improvements.

Community groups often instigated the most innovative new ideas. ISTEA funded projects ranging from the five-mile Coeur d'Alene Lake Drive Bike Trail in Idaho to the refurbishment of historic downtown Owensboro, Kentucky, and pedestrian improvements on the main street in Morristown, New Jersey. Think of the possibilities in your own community.

ISTEA's emphasis on other modes of transportation proved to be popular, and the program was expanded in 1998 and again in 2005. The most recent legislation breaks new ground with a pilot project, championed by Congressman Jim Oberstar of Minnesota and signed by President George W. Bush, that aims to help people switch from automobiles to bikes, walking, and transit as their primary means of getting around. Four communities — Columbia, Missouri; Marin County, California; Sheboygan, Wisconsin; and Minneapolis, Minnesota — were awarded $25 million each to explore creative ways to lessen dependence on the automobile. They are testing out new ideas, which can later be applied everywhere. In addition, $200 million has been made available to help kids walk and bike to school.

RESOURCES

US Department of Transportation: www.fhwa.dot.gov/ reauthorization/safetea.htm

Safe Routes to School Program: safety.fhwa.dot.gov/ saferoutes/

Minneapolis Projects: www.tlcminnesota.org

Learn from Abroad

Europe offers practical tips for enlivening our own communities

Many folks, when they return home from a vacation in Europe, wonder why North American towns and cities don't offer the same sense of wonder. The conventional wisdom is that foreign cities are so much older, with street plans locked in place before the arrival of the automobile. Yet that doesn't seem to be the whole answer. How does it explain the fact that most European cities end gracefully at some point, giving way to green countryside at their edges, unlike the endless miles of sprawl in North America? How is it that public life and street culture in other countries feel more alive?

It's not just the antiquity of the towns, but also the way people there think about their communities. In fact, many Europeans are worried about the impact increasing auto traffic and creeping sprawl will have on the health of their cities. But rather than accepting these changes as the inevitable march of progress, as many Americans do, Europeans are taking action to maintain the vitality of their hometowns. They are reversing urban decay, reducing pollution, protecting historic neighborhoods, improving transit systems, expanding pedestrian zones, preserving green spaces, adding bike lanes, installing pedestrian amenities, and enacting development guidelines to head off ugly outbreaks of sprawl.

At first, Europe's determination to keep its towns livable seems daunting. You might feel this could never happen at home. But why not? North Americans are an enterprising people, restless in pursuit of improving their lives. If more people knew about successful attempts to make cities in Europe and elsewhere more livable and lovable, they would insist on doing something similar here. Maybe we'd do something even better.

People need to know about the transportation options available in Northern Europe, parts of Asia, and in Latin American cities like Curitiba (Brazil) and Bogota (Colombia). Media and politicians never talk about what we can learn from other countries. That leaves it up to us to spread word about examples from abroad that can help make our communities better. Read up on what's happening around the world. Travel to these places if you can, and bring back stories and photos for discussions, slide shows, and PowerPoint presentations. Take every opportunity at neighborhood gatherings and public meetings to point out what's being done elsewhere and how that might be applied in your own community. Who knows? In a few years, people may be coming from overseas to see what you've accomplished.

Hearing about the transportation network in the Netherlands comes as a shock to North Americans. In Amsterdam, for instance, only 20 percent of people's trips around the city make use of a car. Instead, 36 percent are made on foot, another 31 percent on bikes, and 11 percent on transit. In the Dutch city of Groningen, 47 percent of all urban trips are on bikes, 26 percent on foot, and 23 percent by car. The German city of Munster as well as Copenhagen and other Danish cities come close to matching Groningen's widespread use of alternative transportation.

Voters in Amsterdam approved an ambitious plan to eliminate most automobiles in a three-square-mile section of the city center, an idea later adopted in numerous other Dutch towns. Paris has embarked on a plan to limit auto use, as have Madrid and Rome. London has seen traffic decline thanks

Almost 80 percent of all trips around Amsterdam are made by foot, bike, or transit. That's because Dutch policymakers vigorously pursue solutions to traffic congestion and pollution.

to a congestion charge on cars entering the city center, following up on the success of similar policies in Singapore, and Oslo and Bergen, Norway.

The Dutch are carefully studying and trying to eliminate the obstacles that people report as the biggest barriers to leaving their cars at home. Research shows that people are much more willing to walk or take transit when the pedestrian environment is attractive, so the Dutch are sprucing up train stations and making nearby blocks more pleasant places to walk. Forward-looking transportation planners advocate expanded home delivery of goods and increased availability of public storage lockers, noting that some people stick with their cars because it's difficult to carry and stow belongings when they're biking, walking, or riding transit.

Freiburg, a city of 200,000 in Germany, offers further inspiration. At the heart of the city is a bustling pedestrian zone filled with people strolling between shops, an open-air market, and numerous sidewalk cafés. The city has also built an impressive network of bicycle lanes and was one of the first cities to convert its old streetcars into a modern light-rail system. In the 1970s, people hopped into their autos for 60 percent of all vehicle trips around the city, but cars account for fewer than half of those trips several decades later, with bike use increasing from 18 to 27 percent of all trips, and light-rail moving up from 22 to 26 percent.

Freiburg's success provides a firm answer to American naysayers who contend that people will never leave their cars at home and that what happens in densely populated Old World cities is not applicable to our own spread-out metropolitan areas. Freiburg is one of Germany's fastest-growing cities, with new development stretching across a wide valley. You see packs of bicyclists waiting at red lights in its expanding suburbs, and light-rail trains gliding past single-family homes on ample lots.

RESOURCES

Institute for Transportation and Development Policy: www.itdp.org (This site describes inspiring sustainable-transportation initiatives in the developing world.)

Carbusters magazine: www.carbusters.org (A Prague-based magazine covering global transportation alternatives.)

Green Urbanism: Learning from European Cities by Timothy Beatley (Island Press, 2000)

Carfree Cities by J.H. Crawford (Utrecht: International Books, 2000). The related website www.carfree.com is devoted to innovative communities without cars around the world.

LONDON RECUMBENTS

Bikes for everyone aged 1 to 99

London, England

In 1993, Nigel Frost started renting out bikes in London's Dulwich Park with the idea that everyone should enjoy a bike ride in the park, even those with physical disabilities. His business is called London Recumbents because many of Frost's rentals are recumbent bikes, which allow riders to pedal from a comfortable, reclined position. But 20 different types of bicycles are available, ranging from tricycles and unicycles to special bikes designed to push a baby stroller or a wheelchair, or bikes that seat three, four, or even six people. The wide choice of cycling options has opened up a world of possibilities for people with physical disabilities, vision problems, or impaired balance.

The first London Recumbents location was so successful that Frost took his idea to Battersea Park, where he opened another bike concession in 1999. Battersea Park administrator Jennifer Ullman was won over by the idea that bikes could serve as a social activity for groups of people. "The side-by-side tandems are very popular," she says, "as are the low-rider tricycles, which are now all over the park in the summertime."

London Recumbents' focus on family and children's cycling has made an especially noticeable difference at several schools close to the parks, where students are parking bikes outside in greater and greater numbers. "We believe that a strong cycling presence in any open public space will have a beneficial effect on the environment around it," says Oliver Taylor of London Recumbents, "by providing positive examples of transport alternatives, leading to reduced car use, better health, and reminding local transport planners that cycling is a viable transport choice that must be taken into account."

RESOURCE

London Recumbents:
www.londonrecumbents.com

Everybody should have an opportunity to bike, says Nigel Frost, which is why he rents special cycles to people of all ages and abilities at two London parks.

Chapter 4

Keeping Peace in the Streets

How to assure safety and promote justice

 Stir up some hope

 Touch someone's life

 Take a chance on trust

 Celebrate National Night Out

 Keep watch on what happens down the block

 Stay on top of political issues

 Hit the streets

Stir Up Some Hope

Any neighborhood, no matter how far down on its luck, can be lifted by positive action

Hard-hit communities often face obstacles that feel insurmountable, including crime, poverty, unemployment, discrimination, pollution, and other woes — all of which can crush the spirit of people living there. Despair becomes the biggest problem of all as everyone — inside the community and out — loses faith that anything can change. The most important goal then is to crack through that sense of hopelessness, showing that change is possible.

North Philadelphia stood out as one of the most troubled inner cities struggling with decline in the 1980s. Vacant lots strewn with rubble dominated the landscape — a testament to the economic, social, and psychological devastation of the local community.

That's when Lily Yeh entered the picture. She was an art professor at Philadelphia's University of the Arts, and her friend Arthur Hall, the late dancer and activist who founded the Ile Ife Black Humanitarian Center, invited her to work on a particularly grim stretch of abandoned lots near his dance studio. Yeh was shocked at the state of the neighborhood and didn't quite know where to start. But she knew something had to be done. Together Arthur and Lily developed a small vision to create a park on the lots. This vision began with cleaning up the trash. That drew the attention of local kids, who wanted to know, she remembers, what

"this crazy Chinese lady" was up to. The kids' parents came out to watch too, and Yeh realized she had some collaborators for what was to be the most important art project of her life. Soon everyone was involved in cleaning up the area, painting murals, and creating an "art park," which then became the pride of the community.

Twenty years later, this predominantly African-American neighborhood still has unemployment nearing 30 percent, but the park and neighborhood are vibrant places that have helped residents to think of themselves differently. Lily Yeh's work grew into the Village of Arts and Humanities, of which she was executive and artistic director for many years. The park has become a tangible symbol of renewal that encompasses 17 sculpture gardens, numerous murals and mosaics, green spaces, community parks, performance spaces, a tree farm, and even a playground constructed in collaboration with the Philadelphia Eagles. Six buildings have been rehabbed into workspaces for Village projects, with local residents getting on-the-job training in construction trades. The Village also constructed six new buildings for low-income families who were first-time home buyers. A craft production center was established, and the Village is now involved in a new initiative, Shared Prosperity, that will address economic conditions in 99 square blocks of North Philadelphia.

The Village has created an intensive youth-leadership program that offers education through the arts, a theater program, job training, and summer work placement. Young people involved in the theater program create original plays drawing on their own experiences in North Philly. These plays have been performed at the Village as well as in cities such as Boston, Atlanta, Albuquerque, and Peterborough (New Hampshire). Fall brings the Kujenga Pamoja festival (Swahili for "together we build"), which culminates in an elaborate torch-lit coming-of-age ritual for these hard-working, creative teens.

"One of the most powerful things I learned," Yeh told *Yes!* magazine in 2005, "is that when you ... transform your immediate environment, your life begins to change."

Yeh's observation was seconded by James "Big Man" Maxton, who gave up running drugs in favor of making mosaics for Village projects.

The Village of Arts and Humanities — a twenty-year public art and community self-empowerment project in North Philadelphia — has changed how the city thinks of this low-income area. Founder Lily Yeh works on a mural as volunteers look on.

"[Yeh] wrapped her arms around me and taught me to believe in myself," he once said.

The Village of Arts and Humanities has changed how residents of North Philadelphia think about their home — and how everyone else does too. Philip Horn, director of the Pennsylvania Council on the Arts, notes that it "changed the perception of the [wider] community from 'there's something wrong with these people' to 'there's nothing wrong with these people'."

Union County in South Carolina faced devastation of a different sort. Already struggling with the shutdown of several local textile plants, it found itself in national headlines in 1994 when Susan Smith, a disturbed mother, drowned her two young sons by driving a car into a lake and then concocted a story about a black man committing the crime. Some folks believed her at first, reopening old racial wounds that had divided the community. The incident gave the community a bad sense about itself that lingered many years.

Art Sutton, who owned the local radio station, decided it was time for some healing, so he organized a group to put on a play about Union County. Working with Community Performance, Inc., a theater company from Chicago, local folks produced *Turn the Washpot Down*, a pageant of local stories that didn't whitewash history but at the same time instilled a sense of pride in the community. The show enjoyed 11 sold-out performances and led to the formation of a local theater company, Boogaloo Broadcasting.

"Its potent impact is derived from its truth," wrote critic Linda Frye Burnham in *American Theater* magazine, "the resonance of shared ordeals and delights, its portrait of a place like no other." *Turn the Washpot Down* had a deep influence in the community, Burnham noted. "It has already saved its soul."

RESOURCES

Village of Arts and Humanities: www.pps.org/great_public_spaces

Community Performance, Inc.: www.comperf.com

Boogaloo Broadcasting: www.boogaloobroadcasting.com

Lily Yeh: "Art in the Village," by Abby Scher in *YES!* Magzine

Fighting crime is a walk in the park

Washington DC

For a time, Meridian Hill/ Malcolm X Park in Washington, DC had the dubious distinction of being one of the most violent parks in the region. The low point came in 1990 when a boy was gunned down just outside the park. In response, local resident Steve Coleman called a meeting with his neighbors to stop the violence and reclaim the park. Members of the patrol wore orange hats and carried no weapons but said "hello" to everyone they met in the park. "It's a simple thing, and it sounds corny, but it really works," notes Coleman.

A few of the volunteers decided to venture into the park at night to see what was happening. They were surprised to discover that some of Meridian Hill's nighttime denizens really cared about the park and were keeping an eye on things themselves. Some of those people have since made key contributions to the park's revitalization. One even became the chair of Friends of Meridian Hill, the organization that evolved from the patrol effort. "We found that these people, although they seem intimidating to approach, were phenomenal assets," says Coleman.

As their first official act, Friends of Meridian Hill organized a cleanup. More than 100 people came out in the rain and filled nearly 400 garbage bags with trash. After that initial success, many more projects followed, linking people in the neighborhood to the park through arts events, solstice celebrations, and, incredibly, twilight concerts. Within just a few years, park attendance quadrupled and crime dropped 95 percent. On Earth Day 1994, the Friends of Meridian Hill received the National Park Service's highest organizational honor, the National Partnership Leadership Award, from President Bill Clinton in a White House ceremony.

RESOURCE

Friends of Meridian Hill: www.washingtonparks.net/ meridianhill.html

A concerted effort by nearby residents to reduce violence in the neighborhoods has quadrupled attendance at Meridian Hill/ Malcolm X Park in Washington, DC.

Take a Chance on Trust

Fear of crime is often a bigger problem than crime itself

Neighbors watch out for one another on this block in New York's West Village.

Just north of downtown Des Moines, Iowa, lies a picturesque neighborhood that evokes the charm of the 19th century, with tall trees shading the streets, stately Victorian homes, and easy walking distances to shops and other attractions. Like similar neighborhoods around the country, Sherman Hill is becoming a fashionable address for professionals who want something more than standard-issue suburban homes.

The first middle-class people moving back to Des Moines' Sherman Hill were seen as brave pioneers, venturing into a crime-ridden area. Sniper Hill was what some folks called it. That now sounds ridiculous. Even at the height of the 1980s crack epidemic that swept through medium-sized towns like Des Moines, the crime figures for Sherman Hill would have been greeted with jubilation by residents in inner-city Baltimore or Atlanta or Los Angeles.

This shows what a huge role perception plays in our sense of public safety. There seems to be some urge deep down in the human psyche to stoke our worst fears, to find imminent danger in ordinary situations. Unfortunately, this urge is now exacerbated by sensationalized newspaper stories and local TV news where "if it bleeds, it leads."

Many city neighborhoods and, more recently, inner-ring suburbs are stigmatized as hot zones, where no one should venture after dark — or any time — even though crime stats often show these areas are relatively safe. Problems are exaggerated far beyond reality, leaving the impression that people living there pray in thanks at bedtime they were not mugged, raped, or murdered that day. Yet even in areas with the highest crime rates, people who keep their distance from illegal activity or youth gangs are usually untouched.

Outer suburbs are more dangerous than inner cities according to one study, sponsored by Northwest Environment Watch at the height of the '90s crime wave. When researchers factored in people's chances of being smashed up in an automobile accident, inner cities ranked safer than even upscale new suburbs.

Crime is certainly a problem that no person, no matter how poor, should have to put up with. But in many neighborhoods, the

NATALIE POLLARD

perception of crime is a worse problem than crime itself because it drags down all efforts to fix the situation. A part of town labeled "tough" or "bad" loses faith in itself. The people living there come to see themselves as "losers" and view everyone around them as potential criminals.

Many standard crime-prevention strategies actually thwart efforts to improve the neighborhood by reinforcing these negative perceptions. Bars on the windows, store clerks behind plate glass, police officers questioning anyone who walks down the street, chain-link fences, motion-detector lights, and buildings that resemble fortresses all send a message that this place is trouble. You should strongly question whether such anti-crime measures are truly necessary in your neighborhood. Even if you gain a short-term feeling of security, it might trigger long-term losses in a community's resolve to address its problems and to feel proud about itself.

The startling drop in crime rates in New York City and other US cities in the 1990s is widely credited to a law-enforcement theory, espoused by former New York police chief William Bratton and others, that quality-of-life issues matter a great deal in fighting crime. Once thought by cops to be too small to worry about, such minor infractions as broken windows, graffiti, and uncivil behavior (for example, threatening gestures or public urination) are now seen as the seeds of bigger problems.

You can help fight crime by taking any opportunity to enhance the quality of life in your neighborhood or in struggling areas around your town: pick up litter, turn a vacant lot into a park, grow flowers in your front yard. Gus Newport, the first African-American mayor of Berkeley, California, who later headed an inner-city revitalization program in Boston, extols the importance of "culture, vital businesses, or beauty. If you had those things in the inner city, you'd have a lot less crime .... Beauty — no matter how small it is, just a few flowers — is what matters most."

One of the best investments you can make in your community is to expect the best from people. Plant flowers in the window box, even though someone could easily dig them up. Paint a mural, even if there's a chance that it might be defaced by graffiti. Think twice about installing glaring security lights and other intrusive anti-crime hardware. (Use your best judgment, of course. Leaving the front door unlocked at night is rarely a good idea.) Like any investment, there's a risk involved, but the potential payoff — living in a place where people trust each other and feel optimistic about their community — seems worth it.

RESOURCE

Northwest Environment Watch (now the Sightline Institute): www.sightline.org

Keep Watch on What Happens Down the Block

Folks like you, more than cops and surveillance cameras, make a place safe

In the 1960s, a journalist and neighborhood activist named Jane Jacobs squared off against urban design experts — and forever changed the way we look at cities. Her seminal book *The Death and Life of Great American Cities* debunked the follies of modernistic town planning, especially ill-conceived urban renewal plans that tore down cities in the name of saving them. The sterile projects that were subsequently built on the ruins of poor neighborhoods, she noted, were less vital and more unsafe than the slums they replaced.

Planners fiercely attacked Jacobs, questioning her right even to speak on the subject. After all, she had never been trained as an architect or urban designer. She was merely a writer at an architecture magazine and a mother raising three kids in New York City. But that experience proved more valuable in understanding how communities really work than all the advanced degrees and architectural prizes possessed by celebrated urban planners. What Jacobs saw covering stories for *Architectural Forum* and living day-to-day in Greenwich Village gave her keen insights into how to improve urban communities. When she died in 2006, she was honored all over the world as a visionary in the field.

One of Jane Jacobs' great discoveries is that people on the streets provide more safety than police cars, surveillance cameras, bright lighting, fortress-like architecture, bars on windows, or burglar alarms. "A well-used city street is apt to be a safe street," she wrote. "A deserted city street is apt to be unsafe." While that sounds pretty obvious to us, it was a radical concept to the people responsible for planning North American cities in that era. They were doing everything possible to remove human activity from the streets and then wondering why crime rates were soaring.

One of the safest neighborhoods in America at that time, Jacobs notes, was the North End of Boston. Yet it was considered by many planners to be exactly the sort of crowded, dilapidated, outdated area that needed to be bulldozed (as happened to the nearby West End neighborhood). The North End then was a poor area populated by immigrant Italians and frequented by strangers of all races — all the hallmarks of a "bad" neighborhood in the stereotypes of the time. Yet Frank Harvey, who ran a social service agency in the neighborhood, told Jacobs, "I have been here in the North End 28 years and have never heard of a single case of rape, mugging, molestation of a child, or other street crime." Harvey went on to say that the few times criminals attempted such things, they were immediately thwarted by passersby, shopkeepers, or people yelling from upstairs windows.

This is a perfect illustration of Jacobs' important idea that "there must be eyes on the street." A healthy flow of pedestrians on the sidewalks, as well as residents and shopkeepers watching what goes on in front of their properties, is what makes an area safe. When troublemakers know they're being watched, they don't act. The empty streets of suburbia or upscale city neighborhoods with little activity on the sidewalks, are far less secure than the many alleged "tough" inner-city neighborhoods with bustling streets.

Jane Jacobs' insights can easily be applied to your own neighborhood. Walk, rather than drive, through the neighborhood whenever you can. Sit on the stoop or front porch with your lemonade or newspaper, keeping an eye on what's going on, rather than retreating to the backyard or rear balcony. Move some chairs or a picnic table to the front yard. Even when you are not there, they send a signal that people are keeping an eye on what goes on in this neighborhood.

RESOURCES

The Death and Life of Great American Cities by Jane Jacobs (Random House, 1961)
Jane Jacobs: "Jane Jacobs," www.pps.org

Urban visionary Jane Jacobs reminded us that our "eyes on the street" are more important than police in preventing crime. You can see this principle in action in Boston's North End (above) and Madison, Wisconsin (below).

Simply by taking a walk, you can help keep the peace in your part of town.

Hit the Streets

Lively neighborhoods filled with people are safe neighborhoods

Y ou don't have to be an ex-line-backer or hold a black belt in karate to help keep the peace in your neighborhood. Anyone out on the sidewalks deters crime and brings a measure of harmony to the area. Look for any excuse to step out for a stroll, then make a special effort to greet everyone you meet with a smile and watch out for any signs of problems, like a fresh scrawl of graffiti or unusual comings and goings at a residence.

Grandmothers in the Yesler Terrace public housing community in Seattle helped rid their streets of crack dealers. They set up lawn chairs every evening at corners frequented by dealers. All they would do is knit and chat, but it was enough to drive the troublemakers away. In the nearby Garfield neighborhood, members of the community council declared the area a drug-free zone and led marches through the community on Friday nights to show they were serious.

An effective anti-crime initiative underway in many parts of the country is organizing groups to walk the beat — just like the police used to do in the days before squad cars. Indeed, many cities from San Diego, California to Abilene, Texas, and Charleston, South Carolina, are assigning cops back to the beat, on foot or on bicycles. They patrol the streets to prevent crimes rather than simply answering calls once crimes have been committed.

Police can't be everywhere you need them, especially now when slashed federal and state funding to municipalities mean cutbacks in police protection. But citizens are coming forward to help keep the streets safe by patrolling their neighborhoods.

Neighbors in the Lyndale neighborhood of Minneapolis helped bring crime down 40 percent in four years. Calling themselves the Lyndale Walkers, they walked the streets in pairs or larger groups, strolling up and down the sidewalks of this diverse community that includes elegant turn-of-the-20th century homes and a high-rise public housing project. They rarely stopped a crime in action and never pursued confrontations with young gang members, but they did notify the local police precinct by cell phone whenever they saw something suspicious underway. They also filed reports detailing what they found on their walks, which helped police get a better overall picture of problems in the neighborhood.

Just as important, their simple presence on the sidewalks discouraged lawless behavior and raised hope in the neighborhood. Indeed, in a short time Lyndale went from being a place that prospective home-buyers avoided to being the neighborhood with the fastest-rising property values in the entire state. That's according to Myron Orfield, a law professor and former Minnesota state senator who maps out the cycles of urban decline and revival in neighborhoods across the United States.

The success of the Lyndale Walkers inspired similar efforts in other communities across Minneapolis. Reverend Carly Swirtz, leader of the 11th Avenue Block Club in the low-income Phillips neighborhood, describes her experience. "We have lots of successes. One of the best advantages of a patrol is getting to know your neighbors. You can learn a lot on those strolls! We had two really big problem crack houses a couple of years ago. Many gunshots and police calls. It was due to our block club patrol and watch [group]

that we finally got them out. With much help from the Minneapolis police. It was a Saturday morning when the last tenants were escorted out by the police. A large group of us stood on the corner (robes, slippers and assorted dress!). We all cheered the police."

Neighborhood safety is about more than crime. Luther Krueger, one of the leaders of the Lyndale Walkers, notes that even neighborhoods with quite low crime rates are forming walking groups to promote a sense of community. Nolan Venkatrathnam, a patrol leader in the Stevens Square/Loring Heights neighborhood, which does contend with crime problems, notes that one of their notable successes came when "a patrol team retrieved a woman from her apartment that was filling up with smoke from a frying pan left on the stove. The woman had apparently taken medication and fallen asleep and left the pan on the stove. Well, the patrol got the woman out and [she] was treated by medical personnel. The result of all this was that the patrol team was awarded a resolution from the City Council."

RESOURCES

Garfield neighborhood drug-free zone: Described in *Neighborhood Power* by Jim Diers (University of Washington Press, 2004)

Lyndale Walkers: old.tcfreenet.org/conf/ safetynet/patrol.html

Touch Someone's Life

Becoming a mentor can make a profound difference — especially for you

RESOURCES

Big Brothers/Big Sisters:
   www.bbbs.org

Marc Freedman:
   www.civicventures.org

Mentoring: www.mentoring.org

Leonardo's Basement:
   www.leonardosbasement.org

Center for Health Communication:
   www.whomentoredyou.org

Marc Freedman thought something had gone terribly wrong with his research on mentoring programs. He was shocked by what his data showed about the difference a mentor makes in a kid's life.

Freedman tracked 1,000 children seeking mentors through the well-known Big Brothers/Big Sisters program. The kids in his study were aged 10 to 16; all were from single-parent households, and 80 percent of them lived in poverty. The children were divided into two groups. Due to a shortage of volunteers, only half of them were matched with a mentor. The other half were put on a waiting list. One year later, Freedman examined what happened to the children in each group. He found that kids who had maintained contact with a mentor for the entire year were:

- 46 percent less likely to experiment with drugs
- 52 percent less likely to be truant from school
- 33 percent less likely to exhibit violent behavior

Freedman found one further big surprise in his research. Very few of the mentors had any background in counseling, education, psychology, or youth issues. "It was just the relationship itself," Freedman notes. "They were ordinary people spending 10 to 12 hours a month with these kids, taking them to McDonald's and ball games. It's like that old Woody Allen line: 'Ninety percent of life is showing up.' They showed up for these kids and they listened to them."

You can show up for children in your neighborhood too. Help out in the schools. Coach a sports team. Teach a hobby at an after-school program. Tutor kids who need a boost in math or reading or social skills. Volunteer for youth programs through your church, synagogue, or community center. Contact local social service agencies or Big Brothers/Big Sisters about how you can pitch in.

Leonardo's Basement offers kids a chance to work on their own inventions with knowledgeable adults. This unique program began in Minneapolis when students at Clara Barton Open School felt a need to use their creativity in new ways. They hit on the idea of opening a workshop where they could design and build some of the wild things they dreamed up in their heads. They took this idea to their parents, who helped them make it happen.

Located downstairs from a popular neighborhood coffee shop and named after da Vinci, of course, Leonardo's Basement is a wondrous place brimming with scrap wood and metal, disassembled electronics, and all manner of building materials donated by local businesses and individuals. Kids from Barton School and the surrounding neighborhood get encouragement and one-on-one instruction in how to build their brain-storms.

More than 600 students take part every year, with special efforts made to see that 25 percent of them are from underprivileged backgrounds and at least 40 percent are girls. The creative instructors, as the mentors are called here, include several college students who were among the students who originally dreamed up the idea of Leonardo's Basement.

Chicago journalist Salim Muwakkil notes how he and a few friends stop in for a chat with kids in the neighborhood who look like they are starting to get into trouble. This lets kids realize that adults see what's going on and, more importantly, lets them know there is someone they can talk to who cares about what happens to them.

This kind of engagement can make a difference in any kind of neighborhood. Show an interest in the games and activities of neighborhood kids, especially when they are young. Ask them questions. Share your own interests. Get to know their families and ask permission to take them out for ice cream or give them a guided tour of cool places in the community they may not know about. As important as family is to children, it's also valuable for them to have other interested adults in their lives, especially when they hit the turbulent teenage years.

Growing awareness of the key role non-parental adults play in helping kids is fueling new interest in an old idea: godparents (now sometimes known as co-parents). As every mom and dad knows, raising children is hard and sometimes overwhelming work in modern society, where so many people lead isolated lives. Parents need an occasional break from the kids and, frankly, kids need a break from their parents. Close-knit communities that once naturally provided these opportunities have broken down for most people.

Co-parents can help reweave essential community bonds. It works this way: when a child is born, parents choose several other people willing to commit themselves to being a part of the child's life. This means more than babysitting. It involves forging a close bond independent from the relationship with the parents. Co-parents spend time with the kid regularly and take an active interest in what happens to him or her. Neighbors are ideal for this role since they live close by.

Mentoring is not just confined to young people. Many people of all ages seeking help or inspiration might benefit from what you've learned through the years. Use your career experience to help entrepreneurs and civic organizations succeed. Offer support and ideas to the people teaching in local schools or running social service agencies. In fact, the most valuable expertise you provide might be your own knowledge of the neighborhood.

The beat goes on here in Louisville, Kentucky as kids get drum lessons and an introduction to homegrown veggies.

COMMUNITY FARM ALLIANCE

COMMUNITY FARM ALLIANCE

La dolce bocce

San Rafael, California

A downtown park in San Rafael, California, felt off-limits to most local residents due to the rowdy crowd that gathered there. But when bocce ball courts were added as part of a revitalization plan, it became the most popular spot in town.

At one time, much of San Rafael's downtown Albert Park was colonized by vagrants. Local residents felt unwelcome in their own park and became determined to reclaim it, especially since the park occupied an important location next to the community center. Many citizens came together to forge their own vision for the park at a series of meetings organized by the Department of Parks and Recreation. Ideas ranged from building a porch linking the community center with the park to adding bocce ball courts.

Residents formed committees to implement each element in their plan. When a member of the bocce committee discovered fading photographs of long-gone courts in Albert Park, it presented a golden opportunity to reconnect the city to its heritage. The committee canvassed local bars, restaurants, and shops to raise money for new courts, which resulted in the formation of the Marin Bocce Federation. Federation members surveyed public bocce courts in nearby towns and in San Rafael's Italian sister city, Lonate Pozzolo, to which many local residents trace their ancestry. The city provided seed money to begin construction, while the local community raised funds by organizing bake sales, flea markets, and many other events. Six courts were built, with a delegation from Lonate Pozzolo bringing dirt from Italy to mix into the soil beneath the courts.

Today the courts attract 1,000 people per week for the bocce league, with many more casual visitors and players. Every night, bocce players and their families come from all over San Rafael, bringing picnics. Seniors, who rarely ventured into the park before, have organized a daytime league of their own. A new rose garden and gazebo were added to the park in 2006.

RESOURCE

Marin Bocce Federation:
www.marin.org/community/
MarinBocce/index.cfm

COMMUNITY FARM ALLIANCE

Bringing wholesome food to the inner city

Louisville, Kentucky

More than 90,000 people live in West Louisville, but with just a few grocery stores offering produce sections, residents of this primarily African-American neighborhood must eat mostly processed foods from convenience stores. "None of them carry anything that's green and leafy," says Deborah Webb, executive director of the nonprofit Community Farm Alliance (CFA). Since 2003, the CFA has addressed this shortage by forging partnerships between farmers in rural areas and grassroots groups in West Louisville to create markets.

Two years ago, before setting up a single stall, CFA held a series of neighborhood meetings about food. "We asked people, 'What are your food problems? How could markets help you? How could we create something different here?'" recalls Webb. Following these meetings, residents organized themselves into farmers market committees, which then took charge of managing the new markets: Portland Market, the Rowan Street Co-op, and the Smoketown Shelby Park Market.

The markets have won a loyal following by making food part of a broader overall public experience. The Smoketown Market, held on the grounds of a middle school, entices people with outdoor cooking demonstrations that send aromas wafting through the windows of nearby public housing. The market has also spun off a year-round "Kids Café" that provides children with a freshly prepared meal between lunch and dinner on Saturdays. Webb says, "There is a real fondness for the farmers — a lot of hugs on Saturday."

RESOURCE

Community Farm Alliance:
www.communityfarmalliance.org

Farmers markets in Louisville nourish inner-city neighborhoods with community spirit as well as healthy food.

SUCCESS STORY

Celebrate National Night Out

The Fourth of July commemorates American independence. The first Tuesday of August honors our interdependence with one another

Mark the calendar. The first Tuesday of August is National Night Out, a gala happening that brings out more than 30 million people in 10,000 communities across North America to celebrate their neighborhoods. It's not only a blast — with people gathering for block parties, cookouts, street dances, and parades — it's also one of the best ways to keep your community safe.

The connections people make with one another on this night of fun and festivity carry on through the whole year. We get to know folks on our block or in our building better, and that enables us to better watch out for one another. What was that noise? Who's that strange person in the backyard? Is everything all right over there? Strong social bonds are the frontline defense against crime.

Many neighborhoods mark National Night Out with a block party, often closing off the street to make it a memorable occasion. Kids can move freely on trikes, bikes, scooters, skateboards, and their own two feet. People of any age enjoy taking over the street with barbecue grills and picnic tables for a potluck feast.

In Minneapolis and St. Paul, which usually have the highest National Night Out participation among larger cities, police officers drop by some of the many hundreds of block parties to talk about crime-prevention efforts, and firefighters show up with bright red fire engines to give kids rides.

The Bloomington, Illinois, police department hosts a National Night Out party at Miller Park each year. It is attended by more than 10,000 local residents and features live blues music, games, raffles, karaoke, K-9 police dogs, crime-prevention information, and the opportunity to sign up for neighborhood watch groups that work with the police department on crime problems and prevention in various parts of town.

"The best crime prevention tool is a good neighbor!" announces the city's National Night Out website, explaining that the goals of the event are to heighten crime- and drug-prevention awareness; generate support for, and participation in, local anti-crime efforts; strengthen neighborhood spirit and police-community partnerships; and send a message to criminals letting them know that the city's neighborhoods are organized and fighting back. "Come help create safer neighborhoods, block by block, helping neighbors know each other and celebrate a community effort to fight crime," the police department says.

National Night Out is coordinated by the National Association of Town Watch, an umbrella organization of groups dedicated to the "neighbors watching out for neighbors" model of fighting crime. Project 365 is a new initiative from the organization that encourages communities to designate particular problems they want to fix by the time the next National

Night Out rolls around, in 365 days.

An inspiring story from the small city of Rantoul, Illinois, illustrates the promise of Project 365. The town, which suffered economically after the local air force base closed a few years ago, is home to 13 neighborhood watch groups. One of these groups was organized when residents became frustrated by the activity at a drug house that was terrorizing that part of town. Local resident Mary Kruger reports that neighbors, working with the Rantoul police department, kept a close eye out for "[strangers] looking into windows and parked cars; unusual noises; property being taken out of houses where no one is home or a business is closed; cars, vans, or trucks moving slowly with no apparent destination or without lights; ... a stranger sitting in a car; abandoned cars."

Through neighbors' determined monitoring of comings and goings at the drug house over two months, police were able to acquire enough evidence to shut it down and bring peace back to the neighborhood.

To organize a neighborhood watch group or National Night Out event in your area, contact your local police department. If it doesn't sponsor such a program, contact the National Association of Town Watch.

RESOURCES

National Night Out & National Association of Town Watch: www.nationalnightout.org 1-800-NITE-OUT

National Night Out in Bloomington, Illinois: www.bloomingtonnational nightout.com

Rantoul, Illinois, drug house success story: www.nationalnightout.org/ nno/p365story_kruger.html

Any event that brings people out, like this Bastille Day celebration in Brooklyn, forges community connections that continue throughout the year.

Stay on Top of Political Issues

No neighborhood is an island. What happens in city hall, Washington, DC, and corporate boardrooms affects your place in the world

The emergence of strong neighborhoods shaping their own futures is an exciting development in today's democracy. It's common sense that most social problems are best solved close to home. Faraway bureaucrats and faceless corporate functionaries who've never set foot in the neighborhood are in no position to know what will work where you live. You and your neighbors are the world's foremost authorities about your own community.

Yet as much as you might wish to ignore what happens in city hall, state and provincial capitals, Washington, DC, Ottawa, and corporate headquarters, you simply can't. Outside political and economic forces set the rules and shape the events that your neighborhood must deal with every day. **What happens across the street is often linked to policies enacted by distant decision makers.** Some people, for instance, point to the slashing of social programs in the early 1980s as the root cause of the serious crime waves that spread across American cities a few years later. Others target the big-business practice of shifting jobs

from inner cities and blue-collar towns to low-wage plants outside the country. Liberals are quick to point out that crime dropped dramatically a few years after Bill Clinton became president and instituted key measures to boost economic prospects in low-income communities. Conservatives, meanwhile, counter that it was permissive attitudes toward criminals and drugs, along with a lowering of moral standards, that fueled the problems, and that tough-on-crime legislation solved the problem.

That debate will not be settled any time soon, but with violent crime rates climbing again in many places, it's clear that people of all political persuasions must raise this and other concerns on the local, state, national, and even international level. There are many methods we can use to make politicians and business leaders aware of the urgent need to bring peace back to our streets, ranging from sponsoring candidates' debates on public safety to circulating petitions to holding peace rallies at the sites of senseless violence.

For the good of your neighborhood, keep abreast of national issues and tell others about what's happening.

Where the teens are

Cleveland, Ohio

The best parks attract people of all ages. If any age group feels excluded, be it 20-somethings or senior citizens, then the park is not truly serving the whole community. In Cleveland, Ohio, the challenge has been to make parks matter to teenagers. A local non-profit called ParkWorks took up this cause in 2002 when it established the Teen Liaisons program.

At the time, ParkWorks already had a track record for programming successful events and activities in many Cleveland parks. "We had an easy time attracting young children — three to twelve years old," notes Nora Romanoff of ParkWorks. "But there was a deficit in attendance from teenagers." Teenagers often found nothing they wanted to do in the parks, so they resorted to loitering and inappropriate behavior. ParkWorks decided to ask teenagers how parks could become better attractions for young people. And the organization didn't stop there; it also hired teenagers to manage park programs for their peers. So began the Community Park Teen Liaisons.

Each Teen Liaison is assigned to one neighborhood park and paired with a local community organization. The liaisons are paid a stipend and given a budget with which to organize events like music performances or kickball tournaments. "Offering these events to the community allows residents to recognize how important the park is to our neighborhood," says Elizabeth Kiousis, a former Teen Liaison who programmed events for Herman Park in the Detroit-Shoreway neighborhood.

The program not only increased teens' use of Cleveland's parks; it also increased the respect children and adults felt for teens in the neighborhood. Now when younger children show up in the park, teenagers take on leadership roles. "It's a double-edged sword, because teens are no longer able to be kids when children are there," adds Romanoff. "But it also shows what can happen when teens are given a place, something to do, and a measure of responsibility."

RESOURCE

ParkWorks: www.parkworks.org

A program in Cleveland gets teens excited about local parks by putting them in charge of activities for younger kids.

Chapter 5

Where the Action Is

How to boost local economic vitality

 Transform your neighborhood into a village

 Think globally, cook locally

 Eat, drink, and be merry

 Turn around your neighborhood business district

 Become a loyal local customer

Transform Your Neighborhood into a Village

We all want to live somewhere lively where it's easy to walk to stores and public spaces. But, sadly, these kinds of neighborhoods are illegal under many modern zoning codes

One of the worst ideas ever to hit American society was the belief that homes, shops, and workplaces should be strictly segregated from one another. Devised around the turn of the 20th century, when it did make sense in a few cases to locate noxious factories away from schools and apartment buildings, this concept of "single-use zoning" took off to a ridiculous degree after World War II, when corner stores, offices, and even diners were deemed a threat to nearby neighborhoods.

The legacy of this mania for single-use zoning is that many neighborhoods across the continent are now alarmingly dull, with no place to go, nothing to do, and no one to see. But, more and more people are coming to appreciate the advantages of being able to shop and work the same place they live, especially now that the vast majority of workplaces are far more benign than they were at the height of the industrial age.

As we become more anxious about worsening traffic congestion, proliferating sprawl, rising gas prices, global warming, and our expanding waistlines, it only makes sense to arrange our lives so we can meet many of our daily needs without climbing into a car. That was the natural pattern of human settlement throughout history until about 1960.

All great neighborhoods the world over function as villages. Miami architect Andrés Duany, designer of Seaside,

Florida, and other celebrated new communities, defines a village as a place where many of the needs of daily life — a grocery, a school, a café, a hardware store, a park, a child-care center, a transit stop, and perhaps an ice-cream shop, library, or video store — are within a five-minute walk of home. Look around your own town and you'll find that neighborhoods with these amenities are usually the most desirable and often the most expensive places to live.

Duany, along with other leading architects such as his partner Elizabeth Plater-Zyberk, Peter Calthorpe and Daniel Solomon in San Francisco, and Elizabeth Moule and Stefanos Polyzoides in Los Angeles, launched the New Urbanist architectural movement dedicated to these ideals. Over the past 15 years, New Urbanism has begun to change the face of North America as successful suburban and urban developments in nearly every state and province prove people's desire to live in communities where you can walk to the grocery store.

An even bigger trend breathing new life into city neighborhoods is the resurrection of local shopping districts. What were once soda fountains and haberdasheries, and later vacant storefronts or makeshift apartments, have become restaurants and stores once again. Entrepreneurs, many of them recent immigrants or young people, are leading this charge to revitalize commercial streets in inner cities and inner suburbs.

But these entrepreneurs depend on the help of local citizens as customers and as advocates. Often they need neighbors to turn up at zoning hearings or neighborhood leaders to lobby city council to overturn regulations that stand in the way of community revitalization. Archaic laws might prohibit the kitchen expansion necessary to turn an old delicatessen into a new bakery, for instance, or zoning codes demand a bookstore provide a parking lot even though the overwhelming majority of its customers walk there. These kinds of out-of-date laws can be the biggest deterrent to the revitalization of urban neighborhoods.

Brooklyn, once a place in the shadow of Manhattan, has become a showcase of what's possible for enlivening old neighborhoods. Brooklynites now proudly boast they've no real reason to cross the bridge because everything they want is right down the block. Seventh Avenue in Brooklyn's charming Park Slope area represents the ideal of an urban shopping street, lined with locally owned stores. For a walk on the hipper side, try the funky new bars and cool shops on Smith Street in Carroll Gardens and Cobble Hill. For an ethnic flavor, check out Fifth Avenue in Sunset Park with its flowering of new Mexican, Ecuadorian, and other Latin American businesses.

RESOURCES

Congress for the New Urbanism: www.cnu.org

Andres Duany: www.dpz.com

New Urban News: www.newurbannews.com

Brooklyn: www.pps.org/info/city_ commentaries

Old World villages, with lively local shops and street life, offer inspiration for people working to improve their neighborhoods. This area in Amsterdam, Netherlands delightfully fits the definition of an urban village.

Eat, Drink, and Be Merry

The heart and soul of any community is the local diner, coffee shop, bistro, or tavern

Littleton, New Hampshire, had a great Main Street diner. It was the spot where folks gathered to talk, relax, and share a few laughs. When a series of meetings were convened for citizens to discuss ways to improve their town, some of them took place right in the diner. That reminded everyone of how important public places are to the soul of a community. So they produced T-shirts that summed up their ideas about what makes America great:

RECIPE FOR AN AMERICAN RENAISSANCE

- Eat in diners
- Ride trains
- Put a porch on your house
- Shop on Main Street
- Live in a walkable community

A waitress at Monty's Blue Plate Diner on the east side of Madison, Wisconsin, confirms the Littleton motto when she observes, "One day, as I waited on two booths that were sharing a conversation between them about the latest city council meeting, it dawned on me. Our customers were also hungry for community."

Think of England with no pubs. Italy with no espresso bars. Mexico missing its cantinas. Interesting neighborhoods around the world always offer people places to have a meal or enjoy a drink. The lifeblood of nearly every community is a congenial local joint where you can sit down with friends and neighbors to pass the time and find out what's going on around town. It may not be fancy. It might not even serve the greatest food. But it will be filled with life. That's why the coffee shop boom that has recently swept North American towns, large and small, makes such an important contribution to our civic culture.

Dooney's Café in Toronto is the center of the universe. At least that's what people who live in the vicinity of Bloor Street think — people like Brian Fawcett, who gave his book of essays *Local Matters* the subtitle "A Defence of Dooney's Café and other Non-globalized Places, People, and Ideas." He spends most mornings there drinking coffee or having breakfast and believes it's critical to our mental health that all people have access to a place like Dooney's.

We all might do well to adopt the German custom of a *stamcafé,* which means a restaurant or tavern in the neighborhood that we can call our own. It's what we all saw in the wildly popular television show *Cheers*, but instead of vicariously experiencing this comforting sense of belonging on TV, put on your coat and find the real thing. Better Together, an organization devoted to strengthening communities by strengthening community ties, suggests persuading your local café or tavern to designate one table, preferably a big one, for residents who want to share a conversation with their neighbors.

Architectural theorist Christopher Alexander feels so strongly that bars and restaurants are important to our lives that he included them in one of the precepts in his classic design "bible", *A Pattern Language*. He writes that we need "somewhere in the community at least one big place where … people can gather, with beer and wine, music, and perhaps a half-dozen activities, so that people are continually criss-crossing one to another."

One other great and usually overlooked quality of local taverns: you can walk there. Drunk driving is not a problem caused by alcohol alone, but also by urban design. When people become dependent on cars to get everywhere, they drive even when they shouldn't. Who knows what percentage of drunk-driving tragedies could be prevented if everyone had a bar within walking distance. For ages, people who had one drink too many stumbled home from bars, not endangering anyone except, perhaps, themselves. But the situation changes drastically when the bar is far away, not just around the corner.

RESOURCES

Littleton, New Hampshire: www.golittleton.com

Monty's Blue Plate Diner: Eve Tai's essay "The Blue Plate Special" is in the book *In My Neighborhood: Celebrating Wisconsin Cities* (Prairie Oak Press, 2001)

Local Matters by Brian Fawcett (New Star Books, 2003)

Dooney's Café: www.dooneyscafe.com (More than a website about a neighborhood hangout, it's an idiosyncratic and vibrant website about life in Toronto, Canada, and the world.)

Better Together: www.bettertogether.org

A Pattern Language by Christopher Alexander (Oxford University Press, 1977)

A local eatery is always the spot to see and be seen.

Bright lights, fun city

West Palm Beach, Florida

The City of West Palm Beach, Florida, revitalized Clematis Street, its main thoroughfare, and then tackled a problem many cities face today: a downtown that empties out after the offices close at six. The city's Community Events Division (CED) launched Clematis by Night, a weekly event that features live music with lots of good food and drink. The event, which was designed to overcome people's reluctance to go downtown, drew crowds from throughout the metropolitan area to the city's most important public space, Centennial Square, located at the foot of Clematis Street in front of the public library. Clematis Street is closed to traffic during the event.

The main activity is a concert series that features local and regional musicians playing styles ranging from blues and jazz to rock and reggae. Attendees can buy a variety of regional and ethnic foods, and more than 25 local art vendors and craftsmen are also on hand selling their creations. The CED set up a program enabling local nonprofits to raise funds by staffing the two locations where beer is sold and taking home a percentage of the sales. In the early days of Clematis by Night, the CED relied on the nonprofits to bring their constituencies to the event each week.

Today, between 3,000 and 5,000 people regularly attend on nights with good weather. The economic impact on the area has been tremendous, with 42 percent of attendees also visiting downtown merchants. It has been a welcome supplement for local nonprofits. Since the event started in 1995, beer sales have netted over $600,000 for participating groups.

"It was the most natural way of bringing diverse groups together," says former West Palm Beach Mayor Nancy Graham, who helped spearhead the effort. "It was a party that, from the beginning, attracted people of all ages, races, neighborhoods to come downtown."

RESOURCE

Clematis by Night:
   www.clematisbynight.net

A festive party held Thursday evenings along Clematis Street — in the heart of West Palm Beach, Florida — attracts thousands, including many suburbanites who would never otherwise think to come downtown. It's been a great boost for local merchants.

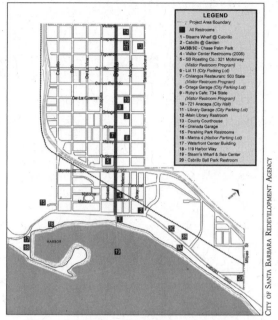

CITY OF SANTA BARBARA REDEVELOPMENT AGENCY

users/adm/eli/rda/tmaps/rda_restrooms.pdf

LOUIS LAZARINE

A good place to go
Santa Barbara, California

Comfort is a key ingredient in any successful public space. Once people feel at ease in a place, they can loosen up and enjoy themselves. Creating a sense of comfort can mean setting out moveable chairs, providing shade and shelter from the elements, or simply keeping the door to the bathroom unlocked.

That's the idea behind a cooperative arrangement among several businesses in downtown Santa Barbara, California. As the area became an increasingly popular destination, visitors found — sometimes uncomfortably — that the supply of available restrooms lagged far behind demand. When the city government refused to build any, the local business improvement district stepped forward with a proposal to find local establishments that would be willing to open their restrooms to the public.

Most businesses were reluctant to let anyone walk in off the street and use their facilities, but owners of the local bookstores and several pubs saw it as a smart business opportunity. They signed up for the program and received a small fee from the city, which installed signs near the doors of participating establishments indicating that a public restroom was available inside. The locations of the restrooms were also indicated on maps of downtown Santa Barbara.

Businesses that took part found providing public restrooms was well worth the "expense." Sales improved due to increased foot traffic, and very few problems resulted. The ultimate sign of the program's success was that the city joined forces with the downtown BID and built two public restrooms itself.

An innovative program in downtown Santa Barbara, California, offers incentives for businesses that open their bathrooms to the public.

SUCCESS STORY

Become a Loyal Local Customer

The old phrase "use it or lose it" applies especially to neighborhood businesses

Living in a neighborhood — even the swankiest one — with no grocery store, coffee shop, or other businesses is like wearing a nice new suit of clothes without shoes. It looks great, but you can't go anywhere. Local shops, preferably within walking distance, are the centerpiece of any community, the place where you bump into your neighbors and get that satisfying sense of belonging.

These neighborhood hangouts don't need to be fancy or charming. Sometimes their funky, idiosyncratic character is the best expression of your neighborhood's true personality. A messy junk shop run by a lovable eccentric can be more welcoming than a quaint-as-can-be tea shoppe or nostalgically correct soda fountain. Even a plain hardware store with good window displays or a laundromat with comfy benches out front can become a kind of town square that attracts people.

In many small Midwestern towns, a drive-in ice-cream stand is the hot spot for teenagers, while older men in the community wander down to the gas station to drink pop and tell stories. In a lot of African-American neighborhoods, the barbershop and beauty parlor are the social hubs. These may not sound like your idea of exciting places, but to the people who live there, such businesses are as important as sidewalk cafés are to Parisians.

In Oxford, Mississippi, many folks credit a bookstore with helping to heal the city's pride after vicious opposition to the civil rights movement erupted in the 1960s. Square Books, located on Courthouse Square, restored many people's faith that this was a civilized community. It also helped revive the sagging downtown.

"What tends to get lost in the argument over the future of independent stores is that the dangers posed to them by superstores and on-line sellers don't just threaten some quaint form of distributing goods," Rob Gurwitt writes in an article about Square Books in *Mother*

Vital business districts — like Main Street in Littleton, New Hampshire — depend on loyal customers to remain vital.

Jones magazine. "They imperil the fabric of our community life. Real-life stores — their place on the street, the people they draw in, the presence they cast in the community at large — help define their neighborhoods."

It's no secret that local businesses almost everywhere are under siege from mega-malls, big-box retailers and the internet. Everyone who cares even a little about their neighborhood should make a commitment to patronize local businesses, even when milk or duct tape or books can be had more cheaply by driving to a national chain store. Vote with your pocketbook to keep your community vital. You might even find yourself ahead economically when you consider the money you save on gasoline and unnecessary purchases you would never have made if you hadn't set foot in the big box. And you'll be way ahead in terms of community spirit and social enjoyment.

Thankfully, small neighborhood stores are beginning to fight back. Business improvement districts are a well-proven model in which local merchants work together to spruce up commercial streets by adding landscaping and other amenities, fixing up the storefronts, and improving lighting. They can also cooperate on advertising campaigns, special neighborhood events, shared parking facilities, and other improvements.

Many merchants are banding together in an even bigger way by joining independent business alliances (IBAs), which draw public attention to the numerous benefits of locally owned businesses. How often do Wal-Mart and Home Depot buy uniforms for the local little league team or sponsor an art fair? Some of these new groups are beginning to lobby political officials to oppose tax breaks for big-box stores, and they alert the media to unfair economic tactics used by giant retailers. The first IBA began in Boulder, Colorado, in 1997 and within two years involved 150 local businesses. There are now IBAs in more than 20 communities — stretching from Corvallis, Oregon, to Greenville, South Carolina — and a national group, the American Independent Business Alliance, based in Bozeman, Montana.

In Hartland, a village in the Devon countryside of England, a community school took over management of the Happy Pear market when the store was about to close. It now offers students an opportunity to learn about business management and sustainable economics, and the store's continued existence means that local townspeople don't have to drive many kilometers for fresh and organic food. This is just one of a growing number of community initiatives to preserve and promote essential local shops. In another English village, Maiden Bradley in Wiltshire, 60 percent of residents pledged between £5 and

£500 ($10 to $1,000) to save and refurbish their general store ("village shop" in the British parlance). It is now community-owned, and any profits go back to the village itself.

Residents of Powell, Wyoming, afraid that a nearby Wal-Mart would decimate their main street, also took matters into their own hands by creating Powell Mercantile, a clothing store owned by 500 local citizens. The store has instilled new life in downtown Powell, and several other new businesses have opened up. Powell borrowed the idea from Plentywood, Montana; and now Worland, Wyoming, has done the same thing. Groups of people from the Wyoming towns of Torrington, Riverton, Newcastle, Rawlins, and, across the border, Ely, Nevada, are closely studying the idea.

RESOURCES

Business Improvement Districts: "Business improvement district" www.pps.org

Square Books: www.squarebooks.com

American Independent Business Alliance: www.amiba.net

Community-supported business: "Community-supported local business" www.globalideasbank.org

Kid's day

Amsterdam, Netherlands

Every April 30, a unique cele-bration occurs in the Netherlands to honor the Queen's birthday. Parties are held everywhere, as people throughout the country don orange clothes in a tribute to the royal family, the House of Orange. But what truly makes this holiday unique is an ingenious legal quirk: All street trade becomes unregulated for one day. This means that musical performers and street artists can be found entertaining people on every corner and square. Above all, it means the streets are taken over by enterprising children. Kids are encouraged to sell whatever they want, wherever they want — on sidewalks in front of

their homes, in parks, or anywhere they see fit.

Taking advantage of this special privilege, children congregate in impromptu "markets" and hawk their wares en masse. One of the most celebrated children's markets takes place in Vondelpark, located in the center of Amsterdam, where children (and their parents) spend the day selling used toys and clothing, performing for passersby, playing games, and picnicking. Over the course of the day, it becomes clear that the celebration is not just about selling things, but about giving kids a public forum to explore their natural creativity.

The Dutch celebrate the Queen's birthday with children's markets, where young entrepreneurs sell their wares, and budding performers showcase their talents.

Think Globally, Cook Locally

Food grown close to home simply tastes better — and dishes up other benefits, too

Modern society has enriched us with remarkable material advantages, but it sometimes robs us of meaning and connection in our lives. This is often apparent at the dinner table, where we sit down to food that has come from God knows where. The vegetables on our plates may have traveled across the country and the fruit halfway around the world, while our meat was produced at a factory farm and the microwave dessert was created in a laboratory.

Eating this sort of food each day raises serious nutritional and social issues, which are now being widely debated. But one thing we know for sure: packaged food shipped into Wal-Mart, Safeway, or other supermarket chains never tastes as good or feels as satisfying as a meal made with locally grown ingredients. Whether it's from a backyard garden, a public market, a community-supported agriculture program, or truck farmers in the area, local food nourishes our souls as well as our stomachs. And it makes a very real contribution to the vitality of our local economy.

Happily, the last few years have seen a boom in local foods, most significantly with the increasing number of farmers markets in almost every community.

"Markets are one of those rare places where all kinds of people feel comfortable," says PPS senior vice president Steve Davies. "People may come here first for food, but they come back for the community. In fact, studies have shown that, on average, people have over 20 social interactions at a market compared to one or two at a supermarket."

The Farmers Market in Athens, Ohio (population 21,000), each Wednesday and Saturday attracts thousands of folks to check out more than 100 vendors of produce, prepared foods, and crafts. The market's motto is "Your dollars go the furthest when they stay close to home." Madison, Wisconsin (population 200,000), also feels like a small town on Saturday mornings when it seems half the town comes to the downtown square for the Dane County Farmers Market.

Besides instilling community spirit, a number of markets are pursuing ambitious goals in public health and economic revitalization.

The Camden Community Farmers Market in economically struggling Camden, New Jersey offers health services and nutrition counseling right alongside heaping piles of wholesome fruits and vegetables. The People's Grocery in Oakland, California, is a literal moveable feast — a portable market that brings healthy, homegrown food to schoolyards and community centers in poor neighborhoods of this predominantly African-American and Latino city. Oakland's Fruitvale Village accomplishes the same thing with a farmers market right outside one of the transit stations

on the BART train line and an adjacent indoor public market.

In Espanola, New Mexico, a Monday farmers market has provided a boost for the economy because local growers now have steady customers for their fruits, vegetables, and chilies. They no longer have to chance a trip to the touristy markets in far-off Santa Fe. The market is also a boon for residents because stores in this low-income town of 15,000 offer little fresh produce.

Panorama City, California, a largely Latino enclave northeast of Los Angeles, has transformed an old shopping center into a mercado-style market as a lively and local alternative to a Wal-Mart across the road.

In Detroit and elsewhere, the story is not just farmers in the city, but farms as well. Enterprising gardeners are moving onto many of Detroit's abandoned tracts of land, producing everything from salad fixings and eggs to alfalfa and goat's milk. In the heart of Stockholm, Sweden, an organic farm grows vegetables, herbs, flowers, and apples. But Burlington, Vermont, takes the prize with 6 percent of the fresh produce consumed in this chilly northern city grown at a 260-acre organic farm right inside the city limits. The farm was once a dump and junkyard but has been reclaimed by the non-profit Intervale Center.

RESOURCES
Farmers markets:
 www.pps.org/markets
Intervale Center:
 www.intervale.org

Shoppers delighted by the green beans at a farmers market in suburban New Rochelle, New York.

Turn Around Your Neighborhood Business District

The remarkable renaissance of Boston's Dudley Street shows the ability of a lively main street, as well as housing improvements, to restore a community's spirit

In the 1980s, Dudley Street in Boston's low-income Roxbury neighborhood seemed an unlikely candidate to become a symbol for urban resurgence. It suffered from all the usual problems of inner-city neighborhoods: poverty, crime, drugs, unemployment, racial discrimination, inadequate public services, run-down houses, poor schools, and redlining (banks' blanket refusal to loan money to anyone in the area). On top of that, the Dudley Street neighborhood had its own unique and daunting problems. More than 20 percent of land in the neighborhood was vacant thanks to widespread arson — a lot of it committed by landlords seeking to collect insurance money. Many of those lots became dumping grounds for truckloads of trash from garbage haulers who used the neighborhood as an illegal transfer station. With many African-American residents and immigrants from the Caribbean and Cape Verde Islands, ethnic and language divisions hindered efforts to organize the community to stand up for its interests.

Against all these odds, Dudley Street now stands as a shining success story of how a neighborhood can turn itself around. Dudley Street itself, once blighted, is now a bustling main street with locally run shops and a town common complete with a farmers market. The nearby Vine Street Community Center features a technology lab, gym, youth center, and dance studio.

This is New England, and you can sense some of that fabled community spirit that Massachusetts' artist laureate Norman Rockwell depicted in his famous paintings and *Saturday Evening Post* covers. Instead of tidy frame homes behind white picket fences, there are rehabbed row houses. In place of a corner soda fountain stands the Ideal Sub Shop, featuring a taste of the Cape Verde Islands (a former Portuguese colony off the coast of Africa). Conversations may be in Spanish, Cape Verdean Creole, or the melodious rhythms of the Caribbean rather than a Yankee accent. But it still resembles the idealized America many of us long for, where kids stop off for candy at Davey's Market after school and folks gather for summer concerts at the bandstand on the town common.

The business district is the heart of Dudley Street's revival. It all began in the mid-1980s when the local Riley Foundation expressed interest in helping the neighborhood and drafted a typical plan inviting outside experts to come in and help the "underprivileged" folks. But those folks would have nothing of it. If they could not run the redevelopment plans themselves, they weren't interested. The Riley Foundation courageously agreed to fund a community-led revitalization effort, and that's how things got rolling.

In a series of visioning sessions, residents expressed their hopes of creating an urban village

— a concept now in vogue among urban planners but quite unexpected from poor and immigrant people, who supposedly care only about "practical things" like affordable housing and new jobs, not frills like a town common. "These people didn't get their ideas from academics. What you have here are a lot of people who grew up in the rural South and the Cape Verde Islands and the Caribbean," says Gus Newport, who helped carry out the community's vision as director of the Dudley Street Neighborhood Initiative. "They don't want to live in tall buildings. They want to know their neighbors. They understood all by themselves that they wanted to get back to the village."

At community meetings, residents' dreams for Dudley Street were recorded on big sheets of paper and taped to the walls. "People Walking. People Talking. People Laughing. Saying Hello to Everyone We Meet" was a typical comment, along with "I want affordable housing and schools with beautiful green playgrounds."

The Dudley Street Neighborhood Initiative was formed in 1985 to turn this vision into reality. Over the past 20 years it has boosted the revitalization of the neighborhood, guided the revival of the business district, and created the town common, as well as building new parks and playgrounds, constructing 400 new homes, rehabbing 500 others, and bringing hope and opportunity back to Roxbury in the form of an urban village.

RESOURCES

Dudley Street Neighborhood Initiative: www.dsni.org

Streets of Hope: The Fall and Rise of an Urban Neighborhood by Peter Medoff (first director of DSNI) and Holly Sklar (South End Press, 1994)

Holding Ground: The Rebirth of Dudley Street, a documentary film by Leah Mahan and Mark Lipman (New Day Films, 1996)

Local residents happily pose at Dudley Street's town common after a successful walkathon to raise money for neighborhood programs.

DUDLEY STREET NEIGHBORHOOD INITIATIVE

Chapter 6

Greening the Neighborhood

How to keep things clean, green, and natural

 Save the planet in your own backyard

 Wage a guerrilla gardening campaign

 Pick up the litter, paint over the graffiti

 Protect the planet by creating some excitement around town

 Form an eco-team

 Reclaim cemeteries as public places

 Plant a forest along your block

Save the Planet in Your Own Backyard

Local efforts are the backbone of green activism

We generally think of environmentalists rallying to save rainforests, coral reefs, deserts, and other faraway tracts of wilderness. But that's just one aspect of saving the Earth. Many green activists stick closer to home, working together with neighbors on important projects in their own backyard. This might well be the kind of ecological action that appeals to you.

PPS itself grew out of the environmental movement. "When I coordinated New York City's first Earth Day celebration in 1970," notes PPS president Fred Kent, "I hoped that the new idea of environmentalism would launch a robust citizens' movement to create what today we would call 'livable' and 'sustainable' communities."

But today we usually view the environmental movement as dominated by lawyers and scientists, Kent notes, not by people working in their neighborhoods. "While environmental organizations have made great contributions, we are increasingly confronted by problems that transcend science or law, from the deterioration of our landscape at the hands of out-of-control sprawl to the decline of once-vital communities in cities, suburbs, and small towns. These realities are shaping the lives of tens of millions of Americans. Many of these people would be willing to stand up as part of the environmental movement if its leaders would address these problems in meaningful ways."

We can enlarge the usual definition of environment to include the places we call home — where we all live and work and play. Indeed, this kind of environmentalism would preserve natural places and human communities at the same time, since improving life in existing neighborhoods means that people feel less urge to move on to new homes in sprawling subdivisions carved out of forest, marsh, desert, or farmland.

This would nurture a new breed of environmental activists working to make busy streets safer for children. They would lobby for sidewalks and neighborhood parks and pleasant tree-lined streets. They would transform outdated shopping malls into neighborhood centers complete with housing, lively public squares, sidewalk cafés, convenient transit stops, and libraries or new schools. This way, malls would become the true community institutions we always wanted them to be.

These dreams don't sound like the stuff of an environmentalist campaign, but why not? All these actions will lead to more walking and less driving, a simple equation that yields large ecological benefits in terms of pollution, climate change, and land use. In fact, creating more congenial *human* environments is one of the most effective ways to curb sprawl, reduce vehicle trips, and rein in global warming.

Leading UK Green campaigner Jonathon Porritt

believes environmentalists must emphasize a sense of place as an integral part of their philosophy. "Most people think the environment is everything that happens outside our lives," he says. "Yet this is a huge philosophical error creating a false divide between us and the physical world. We need to … acknowledge that the environment is rooted in our sense of place: our homes, our streets, our neighborhoods, our communities."

A great opportunity now exists for the environmental movement to reach out to a broader base and new partners simply by expanding the scope of places it is willing to fight for. This expanded notion of the environment would encompass rural watersheds and town squares, coastal wetlands, and neighborhood playgrounds. It's a winning strategy to revive the movement and restore our planet. Let's bring the environmental movement back home to inner cities and small towns and suburban neighborhoods.

You can easily become a part of this exciting emerging movement by just looking around your own neighborhood to see what special places — parks, gathering spots, natural amenities, quiet nooks, play areas, walking routes, business centers — deserve to be protected or regenerated.

RESOURCES

Jonathon Porritt:
    www.greenfutures.org.uk

Protecting the environment means more than saving rainforests and coral reefs. This girl is doing her part working in a community garden.

Pick Up the Litter, Paint Over the Graffiti

Cleanup campaigns restore community pride, setting the stage for bigger improvements

Any American growing up in the 1960s or '70s remembers the motto "Don't Be a Litter Bug." You couldn't miss it on billboards, television commercials, and magazine ads everywhere. Yet widespread cynicism greeted this early effort to clean up the environment, especially First Lady "Lady Bird" Johnson's campaign to "Beautify America." Humans, after all, had been tossing junk on the ground since Neanderthal times. Why would they suddenly stop?

But, surprisingly, it worked, and the amount of litter declined dramatically in a short period. Indeed, the Beautify America campaign helped pave the way for the ecology movement a few years later, and sociologists now point to it as firm evidence — along with smoking bans in public places and pet owners' willingness to scoop up their dogs' poop — that longstanding human behavior can be altered through spirited public education campaigns.

The focus of the litter bug campaign was on personal responsibility. It wasn't until the late 1980s, when President George H.W. Bush was trumpeting the value of volunteerism, that the emphasis shifted to picking up other people's trash — as seen by the sudden appearance of signs along many American highways announcing that a particular stretch of pavement was being kept tidy by "the Muntz family" or "Local 169 of the United Electrical Union."

That effort was successful, too, as garbage disappeared from many roadsides.

These strategies will also work in the streets around your house. Make a habit of bringing a bag along on walks so you can pick up soda pop cans, windblown newspapers, and whatever other junk accumulates on the sidewalks. The next step is to expand the cleanup into a neighborhood-wide project, maybe sponsored by a convenience store or fast-food restaurant — businesses that are probably responsible for a good share of the litter in your area. The sponsors could print up special bags in which to gather the trash and offer prizes to the kid who collects the most.

Residents of Urbana, Illinois, celebrated Earth Day one year by cleaning up Boneyard Creek, netting tons of trash. The creek had been notoriously polluted for centuries, dating all the way back, legend has it, to a Native American graveyard along its banks (hence the name). But the cleanup campaign prompted people around town to think of the creek differently, and soon government authorities began to enforce anti-dumping laws that had been ignored for years because nearly everyone viewed it as an open sewer.

In Baltimore, Maryland, neighbors were worried about the fate of Mount Vernon Place, a four-block inner-city park that was neglected and little used. They organized a group, Friends of Mount Vernon Place, to revitalize the park, and one of their first projects was sponsoring several cleanup days. This helped launch bigger things, such as a flower market and a book festival. Soon the park was getting more attention from city maintenance crews, and eventually a master plan for Mount Vernon Place was drawn up and carried out.

Anything unsightly that detracts from the good image and enjoyment of your neighborhood is fair game for a citizen-led cleanup effort. Don't like big and ugly billboards? Contact your elected officials about getting rid of them. Many communities around the country have banned them altogether. Sick of the graffiti defacing walls and bridges? Organize a bucket brigade to paint over it. City officials might even buy the paint. Once you have paintbrushes in hand, maybe you could also spruce up shabby properties in the area. Older residents unable to deal with chipping paint and other upkeep will be thrilled at the offer of help.

Take care of the whole neighborhood the same way you take care of your own property. These little things will restore pride, setting the stage for even bigger improvements.

RESOURCES

Friends of Mount Vernon Place: www.teammetrix.com/fmvp/

Take care of the neighborhood the same way you take care of your own property.

Form an Eco-Team

The more the merrier when it comes to greening your neighborhood

Rather than just talking about protecting the environment, some communities are rolling up their sleeves to get things done

The fact that two heads are better than one has been well-proven throughout history. And when you get a dozen or so heads together — especially if they belong to folks who care deeply about the place they live — the sky's the limit in terms of what can be accomplished. This principle has been demonstrated in neighborhood after neighborhood as people get together to spruce up, clean up, and green up their community.

The concept of eco-teams — five to ten households working together to live more ecologically — took root in the early 1990s as a way to take action on environmental sustainability by reducing overall production of garbage or cutting energy use. More than 40,000 people in 18 countries have now joined eco-teams. Teams usually meet over a period of months to study various approaches to living more sustainably and then help each other implement green strategies,

although each household ultimately makes its own decision on how it wants to live.

Jennifer Olson and Per Kielland-Lund of Madison, Wisconsin, joined one of the eco-teams sponsored by government agencies and local businesses. "We were able to implement many changes in our daily lives that we, for a long time, had wanted to," they note. "It feels good to be part of the solution and not only the problem."

Olson and Kielland-Lund stress that eco-teams go beyond isolated individual actions because members are part of a broader effort. That's also been the experience of other kinds of local groups that come together to think globally and act locally.

A dozen neighbors in Golden, Colorado meet once a month over breakfast to explore local and environmental issues. And it's not just talk for people in the Harmony Village community. Member Dan Chiras, who hosts the discussions in his kitchen, explains in the book *Superbia!* that the group "proposed that Harmony Village residents install solar panels on the roofs of their homes, and that the village use energy-efficient compact fluorescent light bulbs in outdoor fixtures. They routinely write letters to politicians and recently saved a nearby piece of land that was slated for development."

More than 100 residents of the Boundary Street Neighborhood in Portland, Oregon, have become involved in a project to restore native plants along the banks of a local creek. "We've tapped into neighborhood expertise — one guy has a PhD in biology," notes Dick Roy, one of the leaders of the restoration project. "We've taken advantage of all the good energy to make our neighborhood more environmentally stable."

Roy, a retired attorney, and his wife Jeanne, a community activist, have also founded the Northwest Earth Institute, which offers discussion programs to help guide neighborhood groups, religious congregations, workplaces, and other small circles of people that want to make a difference in protecting the planet.

The Northwest Earth Institute currently offers seven different programs — Discovering a Sense of Place; Choices for Sustainable Living; Healthy Children, Healthy Planet; Exploring Deep Ecology; Voluntary Simplicity; Globalization and Its Critics; and Global Warming — that are designed for groups of 8 to 12 who meet once a week for an hour to discuss the book of readings that comes with the program.

RESOURCES

Eco-teams:
www.greendecade.org/ecoteams.html

Northwest Earth Institute:
www.nwei.org

Superbia! 31 Ways to Create Sustainable Neighborhoods by Dan Chiras and Dave Wann (New Society Publishers, 2003)

FEDERICO SAVINI

FEDERICO SAVINI

This park's for the birds

New York's Lower East Side

At first, Anna Magenta and Federico Savini just wanted to clean up their neighborhood park. So much garbage was accumulating in Sara Delano Roosevelt Park, located in New York City's densely populated Lower East Side, that they felt the need to clean it up themselves. Drug dealers and the threat of violence drove people away from the park in the evenings, although it was still widely used by neighborhood kids and families during the day. Soon Magenta and Savini were joined by neighbors and local children, who looked forward to the regular weekend efforts to reclaim their park.

In 1993, Magenta founded the nonprofit Forsyth Street Garden Conservancy, which began landscaping the park's gardens. Then a member of the local Chinese community approached the Conservancy and asked if a special garden could be built for a group of older Chinese men who had been bringing their songbirds to the park. The birds were a special kind of thrush, known in Chinese as hua mei, and the men brought them into the park to sing every morning.

The Conservancy built the bird garden with help from neighborhood children. It is a semicircular area of approximately 2,000 square feet, dense with stone paths, boulders, lush perennials, and small native and Asiatic shrubs, particularly berry-producing plants that attract wild birds.

In nice weather, as many as 30 hua mei fill the garden. Their singing nearly drowns out the rumble of traffic coming across busy Delancey Street. The garden is also used by people doing their morning tai chi exercises, and it serves as a unique gathering place for the bird owners and other neighborhood residents.

RESOURCE

Hua mei bird garden: "hua mei"
www.pps.org

Chinese immigrants on New York's Lower East Side created a unique bird garden, which is now a favorite spot for many in the neighborhood.

A tomato grows in Brooklyn

Brooklyn, New York

Community gardens are especially valuable in neighborhoods where fresh produce is rarely seen in local stores. They give people the opportunity to grow their own delicious and healthy food. Residents of the East New York neighborhood in Brooklyn took their community gardens one step further. They teamed up with four community organizations to start a market called ENY Farms! on a vacant lot donated by the city, enabling urban gardeners to sell produce to other people in the neighborhood.

East New York is a low-income neighborhood with large immigrant populations hailing from South America, the Caribbean, Africa and Russia. The strength of ENY Farms! lies in its ability to adapt to the diverse tastes and skills of local residents. People from the neighborhood run the market, organizing different themes and activities each week to celebrate the many cultures within the community.

More than 45 percent of customers receive food stamps, which fill critical shortfalls in household budgets, so the market has obtained an electronic balance transfer (EBT) machine that allows all vendors to accept the stamps. In addition to expanding access to fresh produce in the neighborhood, ENY Farms! provides growers with an important source of supplemental income.

RESOURCE

ENY Farms!
www.neighborhoodlink.com/org/enyfarms

ENY Farms! provides a low-income community in Brooklyn with homegrown food from urban gardeners.

Plant a Forest Along Your Block

Trees enrich our lives in more ways than we ever realized

If North American neighborhoods ever organized themselves into a huge representative body along the lines of a parliament or congress, there's little question who would be voted Speaker of the House: Dan Burden, founder of Walkable Communities, Inc. He knows as much about what makes neighborhoods livable as anyone alive, having personally worked with citizens from more than 1,700 towns to make their communities better.

Burden tackles a whole range of problems, from crime to traffic to economic vitality, all of which he believes can be fixed by getting people out on the sidewalks. Recently he's come to the conclusion that street trees have a major effect on the vitality of neighborhoods. In a recent paper, Burden outlined 22 benefits of tree-lined streets, including:

- **Slower and safer traffic.** Trees were once considered a danger to passing motorists, but research now suggests that trees make motorists safer. A 2005 study in the *Journal of the American Planning Association* states that "there is a growing body of evidence that the inclusion of trees and other streetscape features in the roadside environment may actually reduce crashes and injuries on urban roadways." Other research shows that drivers go 3 to 15 miles per hour slower on a stretch of road with trees than they do on one without, even when both are on the same road.

- **Less crime.** A tree-lined street naturally attracts more people and a greater level of upkeep and attention from residents and business owners, both of which are significant deterrents to crime.

- **Improved business.** Stores in commercial districts shaded by trees show 20 percent higher income. This should put to rest the old shopkeepers' myth that trees pose a problem because customers can't see their signs or windows.

- **Better pedestrian environment and safety.** No one enjoys strolling along a road with roaring traffic a few feet away. A stand of trees offers an important buffer that enhances the aesthetic and psychological experience of walking. Tree-lined streets not only feel safer, they *are* safer because traffic moves more slowly and trees provide a visual and literal barrier that keeps inattentive or reckless drivers on the roadway.

- **Protection from the elements.** A line of mature trees shields passersby from moderate rains, intense sun, heavy winds, and hot temperatures. There can be as much as 15 degrees difference between shaded and exposed streets. This protects not only people, but also the roads themselves. According to findings from California, asphalt lasts 40 to 60 percent longer when it is shielded by foliage.

- **Reduced energy use.** As anyone growing up in a hot climate knows, trees can be as important as air conditioning in keeping you cool. Street trees shading a house can reduce warm-weather energy bills by 15 to 35 percent. And in a wonderful example of nature's engineering savvy, deciduous trees shed their leaves in the cooler months when you want the sun's warmth to shine through.

Burden recommends planting trees 4 to 8 feet from the curbs and spaced 15 to 30 feet along your block. For an investment of $250 to $600 to plant a tree and maintain it through the early years, Burden calculates each street tree will offer returns of $90,000 through the decades (not counting the considerable aesthetic, natural, and social benefits).

Los Angeles has its own Lorax (a Dr. Seuss character who speaks for the trees). Andy Lipkis is an arboreal activist committed to planting trees in order to revitalize communities and minimize the effects of global warming. As a teenager, he was fired up by the idea of reforesting Los Angeles, and he and his organization, TreePeople, have planted millions of trees all over the metropolitan region since 1973. Their work doesn't stop there. It's much easier to plant a tree than to take care of it, so the organization has begun a program to train citizen foresters to take care of vulnerable young trees.

RESOURCES

Dan Burden: www.walkable.org

"22 Benefits of Urban Trees" by Dan Burden: www.ufei.org/files/pubs/22BenefitsofUrbanStreetTrees.pdf

Andy Lipkis and TreePeople: www.treepeople.org

Tree-shaded streets not only look nice but studies show they promote slower traffic, less crime, business revitalization and are safer for pedestrians and motorists.

Wage a Guerrilla Gardening Campaign

Vacant lots and other neglected places are prime ground for community gardens

Remember Johnny Appleseed, the legendary horticulturist who roamed the countryside sowing seeds that would grow into bountiful apple trees? You can play the same role in your community by planting flowers and even vegetables in the vacant spots no one takes care of. Nature has a remarkable way of regenerating empty lands, and you can help out by tossing a few seeds through the chain links surrounding a fenced-off property, by planting some wild roses in a drab median strip, or by setting out tomato plants alongside a local business that doesn't bother with any landscaping.

There may be programs in your town that encourage this sort of guerrilla gardening, similar to allotments, the carefully cultivated postage-stamp-sized gardens you see along railroad tracks and in other out-of-the-way corners of European cities. If no such programs exist, don't let that stop you from greening the neighborhood with some undercover horticultural work of your own. Check with your local nursery for species that are hardy and need little care in your growing zone.

Or you can go a step further, like some green-thumbed New Yorkers did in the 1970s, by growing gardens in waste lands. The Clinton Community Garden, now a lovely oasis in the heart of the once-infamous Hell's Kitchen neighborhood, began in 1978 when a group of residents noticed tomato plants growing out of the rubble on a vacant lot that had been neglected for years. The property belonged to the city, and the neighbors rented it through a special program, cleared the area, and built paths using bricks they found on the site. They created a serene public garden in the front, while the back portion of the lot was parceled out to local residents who wanted to tend their own vegetables and flowers.

In 1981, the city prepared to sell the site for development, prompting community protests and a grassroots fundraising campaign that collected more than $70,000 to save the Clinton Community Garden as a public park. Many other community gardens, some of them true guerrilla campaigns waged by gardeners who did not have permission to beautify the lots, have since become part of the New York parks system, bringing refuges of green to high-density neighborhoods around the city.

Volunteers at the Clinton Community Garden care for the herb gardens, rose beds, grape arbor, rock garden, Native American medicinal plants, beehive, lawn, shrubbery, trees, paths, and a special display of more than 100 plant species indigenous to New York City. The garden, still a community-run effort, is open to the public from dawn to dusk and hosts picnics, potluck suppers, chamber music concerts, gardening classes, herb workshops, a harvest celebration, art festivals, many birthday parties, and a citywide summer solstice celebration.

RESOURCES

American Community Gardening Association: www.communitygarden.org

New York City Parks Department program for community gardens: www.GreenThumbnyc.org

Clinton Community Garden: www.clintoncommunitygarden.org

Enterprising gardeners across the continent have taken over abandoned land to plant vegetables and flowers.

Protect the Planet by Creating Some Excitement Around Town

Urban density is nothing to fear. When done right, it not only halts sprawl but also enhances your life

One of the most widespread, and sadly mistaken, environmental myths is that living "close to nature" out in the country or in a leafy suburb is the best "green" lifestyle. Cities, on the other hand, are often blamed as a major cause of ecological destruction — artificial, crowded places that suck up precious resources.

Yet, when you look at the facts, nothing could be farther from the truth. The pattern of life in the country and most suburbs involves long hours in the automobile each week, burning fuel and spewing exhaust to get to work, buy groceries, and take kids to school and activities. City dwellers, on the other hand, have the option of walking or taking transit to work, shops, and school. The larger yards and houses found outside cities also extract an environmental toll in terms of energy use, water use, and land use. It's clear that the future of the Earth depends on more people gathering together in compact communities.

There's something in the American experience that resists this truth. City folks have always been viewed suspiciously, going all the way back to Thomas Jefferson's exultation of the yeoman farmer as the repository of virtue and the champion of democracy. Cities are seen as places that have fallen from grace, dens of corruption and vice and filth.

It's time to get over outdated prejudice and honor the people and places that tread more lightly upon the earth. This calls for a celebration of the inner city, the classic small town, the turn-of-the-20th-century suburb, and the growing number of new developments where people live in congenial proximity with one another and enjoy ample opportunities to get around without hopping into a car.

Defenders of wild places, such as the Cascade Land Conservancy (CLC) in Washington State, now stress the importance of cities. Gene Duvernoy, CLC's president, singles out sprawl as a major environmental crisis in the Seattle area. Duvernoy forcefully argues that if people don't feel satisfied and excited about the places they live now, then suburban development will continue its destructive march right up into the foothills of the lovely Cascade Mountains. His message was clear: If you love nature, you have a stake in making sure people love cities, too.

Ron Sher, a sustainable developer and environmentalist in Seattle, adds, "We can't force people to live in cities if they don't want to. So we must make cities places where people want to live." That's why creating compact and congenial urban neighborhoods that are safe, lively, and attractive places is, according to Sher, "a critical environmental issue."

Of course, an urban address doesn't automatically mean a green way of life. City folks are just as capable of squandering resources and

spawning pollution as anyone else. Too many cities, in fact, are modeling themselves on suburbs by fostering auto-dependent, spread-out, sprawl-happy development. Their zoning codes actually prohibit neighborhood stores, apartments, businesses without parking lots, and other great features that make cities exciting and environmentally friendly.

These kinds of bad choices in cities, suburbs, and small towns are driven by a desperate fear of density. What "density" actually means is "compact" or "urban," but it has been twisted to imply horrible traffic, soulless high-rises, and social breakdown. It's inconceivable to many otherwise savvy Americans that denser development could mean anything other than social problems, pollution, and falling property values in their neighborhood.

Many of the most beloved places around the world are really quite dense, including Paris, Sydney, the hill towns of Tuscany, Savannah, Quebec City, most historic neighborhoods, charming small towns, and even

Disneyland once you get inside the gates. We spend a lot of money and precious vacation time to visit these places, which should prove to us that, done right, density becomes a community's greatest asset.

The problem is that almost everyone can easily point to a place where density was not done right. And in nearly every case, what bothers us is not the density of human beings but the density of cars. So the starting point of any effort to make your neighborhood more compact and "green" is to put cars in their place. That doesn't mean you need to ban them (although car-free communities are a growing trend in Europe); you simply stop accommodating their needs every inch of the way. Put pedestrians first and you'll have a neighborhood that will grow more lively and appealing.

Ugly high-rise buildings are the other reason the mere mention of the word "density" strikes fear in the hearts of many people. And the truth is, most high-rises built over the past 50 years deserve that sort of disgust. They suck all the life

The compactness of old neighborhoods — like Palermo Viejo in Buenos Aires — instills an alluring urban energy.

out of the street with sterile service entrances, huge garage doors, and dull parking lots.

But look to Vancouver, Canada, where high-rise architecture has been re-visioned over the last several decades. The city is full of handsome tall buildings that touch the ground in an attractive way that adds to, rather than subtracts from, existing street life. These high-rises also taper toward the top, minimizing the amount of sky and sunshine that is blocked.

The city of Chicago shows that density doesn't have to mean high-rises. Three million people live there in a surprisingly small geographic footprint. Outside of the notorious public housing projects (many of which have been torn down and replaced with scattered site housing) and a narrow stretch of high-rises on the lakefront, the overwhelming majority of Chicagoans live in single-family bungalows, duplexes, four flats, and low-rise apartment buildings. This helps explains why the Windy City gains more applause every year for its lively, green, livable neighborhoods. And, interestingly, one of the area's up-and-coming neighborhoods is the next-door suburb of Berwyn, which has a population density higher than the city itself with hardly any high-rises.

A special feature of Chicago neighborhoods is the granny flat, a small freestanding residence or carriage house in the backyard of a home. Granny flats are a great way to boost the density of your own neighborhood without changing its character. They make housing affordable in two ways. First, the backyard unit itself provides lower-rent housing. Second, the rent paid for the unit helps the owners of the main house with their mortgage payments. And because the relationship between homeowner and renter is close — they are neighbors, after all — there tend to be fewer problems than occur with absentee landlords.

This is just one of numerous time-tested methods of increasing the population of a neighborhood without sacrificing its traditional look. Others include garden or garrett apartments in big houses (which are, unfortunately, illegal in many cities today) and apartments over the store in neighborhood business districts. All of these housing options allow young adults and older people to stay in their familiar neighborhood when they no longer want to live with their families or stay in a big house. (That was the original idea of granny flats.) They also represent the original affordable housing, giving people who work in a pricier neighborhood the chance to live there, even if they can't afford a house. Ideas like these can be included as part of the plan for new developments as well as in revitalization efforts in older neighborhoods.

RESOURCE

Cascade Land Trust:
www.cascadeland.org

© LAURA BERMAN/GREENFUSE IMAGES

© LAURA BERMAN/GREENFUSE IMAGES

The bread oven that revived a troubled city park

Toronto, Ontario, Canada

Jutta Mason, a mother in Toronto, faced a dilemma. She lived near Dufferin Grove Park but was afraid to go there with her children because it had become a hangout for kids who were viewed as the "local toughs." Still, she didn't want to be stuck in her house. Mason debated whether to endure boredom or confront fear. She chose to confront her fear, and in the process made a great difference in her community.

Her approach was simple. She struck up a conversation about the park with her neighbors and asked them how they thought it could be improved. Together they started talking with the "tough" kids, who, as it turned out, also thought the park needed improving. They all worked to make the warming house at the skating rink safer. Then they planted flowerbeds, resurfaced the basketball courts,

and renovated the playground — projects that were all based on ideas from local residents.

One of their most inspired improvements was the creation of a large Portuguese-style bread oven, which members of the neighborhood use to cook community dinners and throw pizza parties. They also constructed a fire circle, and many neighbors now cook meals over the open fire. This outdoor kitchen has become a center of social activity in the neighborhood. Dufferin Grove Park has been turned around, in large part due to the community effort launched by Mason. A new school has even been established next to the park.

RESOURCE

Friends of Dufferin Grove:
www.dufferinpark.ca

A Toronto neighborhood reinvigorated a sense of community by building a Portuguese-style bread oven at a local park. "People rarely pass by the park oven when something is baking without stopping to talk," says Jutta Mason (left), one of the project's organizers.

Reclaim Cemeteries as Public Places

Some of the nicest spots in any town are reserved for the dead. There's no good reason the rest of us shouldn't be able to enjoy them

A comedian back in the 1960s pushed the boundaries of good taste on an album cover by posing on a blanket in a graveyard with a picnic lunch spread around him, complete with a watermelon. How outrageous! How twisted! Yet, when you stop to think a moment, what's so ghoulish about that? Cemeteries often occupy the most lovely settings in town, with lush green lawns and bright, well-tended flowerbeds. Why should all this beauty be locked away behind fences, reserved for the exclusive use of the dead? Cemeteries should be seen as public gardens where anyone can come to respectfully appreciate the glory of nature and ponder the meaning of existence.

That's how they do it in New Orleans, a place where death is not viewed as something entirely separate from life. Just as the city's famous jazz funerals feature upbeat music and joyous dancing to help send off the departed, New Orleans welcomes the public to its fascinating aboveground graveyards. Some city buses even announce the cemeteries as their final stop. The graveyard is also a must-see stop in any tour of Savannah, another city steeped in idiosyncratic charm. That's where the Baroque statues featured on the cover of the bestseller *Midnight in the Garden of Good and Evil* can be seen.

But, unfortunately, in most American cities there are restrictions imposed on the use of cemeteries. Unless you are a bereaved family member or are attending the annual Memorial and Veteran's Day services, stern regulations (no bikes, no food) and vigilant security patrols make you feel unwelcome. I can't imagine the dead would mind people enjoying themselves nearby — not carnival rides or paintball tournaments, but lovers strolling hand in hand or families sharing a sunny afternoon.

A cemetery sits right at the heart of Appenzell, Switzerland, a village high in the Alps. Gates

Cemeteries, like funerals, are for the living.

are open on all sides, and most trips around town seem to lead through the tidy graveyard. This is not at all unusual in Europe, where an old church often stands in the center of town with a cemetery right behind, full of memorials and benches for anyone who wants to reflect a moment or simply rest their feet.

Ross Bay Cemetery in Victoria, British Columbia, welcomes joggers and bikers. There are weekly public tours, special programs for school kids (which help nip vandalism in the bud), and a ghost tour around Halloween.

Public use of cemeteries is even more common in Latin America, where lines between the living and the dead are not as rigidly drawn in people's imaginations as they are in North America. (You get a glimpse of this in the magic realism of authors like Gabriel Garcia Marquez.) The comedian's picnic in the cemetery would be no joke here, since there is a long tradition of taking elaborate meals out to the cemetery to eat in the company of deceased loved ones. It's a big part of the Mexican holiday of the Day of the Dead (November 1 and 2).

North America may not be ready just yet for graveside picnics, although the growing population of Latino immigrants might soon loosen things up. But in the meantime, it's worth exploring what could be done to open this vast treasure of grass, flowerbeds, trees, and impressive statuary and architecture to the public.

Talk to the caretakers or board of your local cemetery. Let them know how much you appreciate the effort they put into maintaining this civic asset and how great it would be if more people could responsibly enjoy it. They might go for the idea of adding a few benches or hosting public events. If they raise fears of vandalism or litter, which are legitimate concerns, point out that having people from the community care about a place and visit it regularly is the best way to prevent trouble and solve problems.

RESOURCES

Ross Bay Cemetery:
 www.oldcem.bc.ca

Chapter 7
Pride in Your Place

How to nurture pleasure and pizzazz

 Become a neighborhood patriot

 Define the boundaries of your neighborhood

 Draw attention to what's special about where you live

 Root, root, root for the home team

 Build on what's good to make things better

 Celebrate your place in the world

Become a Neighborhood Patriot

No one will stand up for your community if you don't

Fred Kent, president of PPS, sings the praises of "zealous nuts" at every opportunity. That is his term for the local heroes who make things happen in communities. These are the folks responsible for the turn-around seen in so many cities in recent years, much more than the politicians, planners, or designers who often claim credit.

"There is hesitation to empower people who seem to care a little too much," Kent notes, "and who may have minimal experience in planning, business, or government. But zealous nuts know more about the places they live and work than anyone else, and therefore their ideas turn out to be the most practical and valuable."

Betsy Barlow Rogers was the spark plug behind the revival of Central Park in New York City in the 1980s. A long-time user of and advocate for the park, she helped organize, and became the first president of the Central Park Conservancy, a nonprofit organization that manages Central Park under an arrangement with the city of New York. The organization raises money from individuals, corporations, and foundations to restore and improve facilities in the park. Kent credits Rogers and the Conservancy for trans-forming the park from a place that most New Yorkers avoided to the beloved and well-used civic asset it is today. Rogers loved the park too much to simply let it deteriorate.

"Community Patriot" is another way to describe zealous nuts. Sam Adams, Thomas Paine, Paul Revere, and Thomas Jefferson stood up for the places they loved in the face of powerful outside forces. You can do the same in your own community by not staying silent

The revival of New York's Central Park was accom-plished by persistent people who would not give up.

when a crisis, an injustice, or a wonderful opportunity arises. Talk to your neighbors. Circulate a petition. Write a letter to the editor. Call the news desk at local radio stations, TV outlets, and newspapers. Spread the word in local churches, synagogues, and mosques. Create a flyer and tie it to every door-knob in the neighborhood. Raise the issue with politicians, civic leaders, and business owners. Start a website. And, most of all, stick with it. The more determined you are and the more people you organize who feel the same way, the harder it will be for public officials and other powerbrokers to keep telling you "no."

But activist campaigns are just one aspect of being a local patriot. There are many other, equally important, ways to show your love for the community.

- Join the local town council or neighborhood board. (If you don't have a community organization, it's high time to start one.) This gives you an inside track in looking out for the community and promoting improvements.

- Become a community correspondent, chronicling local issues and opportunities for a community newspaper, the op-ed page of a daily paper, locally focused websites, or a radio station.

- If you don't like how your community is covered (or not covered) in the media, go out and start your own. It's easy to produce a neighborhood newspaper with today's technology. Even easier and cheaper is a website devoted to everything that's happening (or could happen) in your part of the world. In Prairie Farm, Wisconsin, Jim Hare bought his local newspaper, *Prairie Farm News*, to make sure there was a strong voice for the community. An organic farmer and long-time political activist, Hare has now added the role of editor (and ad salesman) to his job description as a local patriot. In Kontula, Finland, a working-class suburb of Helsinki, local residents produce their own community radio newscasts, which can be heard on a special Kontula website.

- Or you can simply become your community's number one booster, the person who champions all the great people, places, and things around the neighborhood.

RESOURCES

Zealous Nuts:
   www.pps.org/info/bulletin/
   zealous_nuts

Central Park Conservancy:
   www.centralparknyc.org

Prairie Farm News:
   www.topix.net/city/
   prairie-farm-wi

Radio Kontula: www.kontu.la

Draw Attention to What's Special About Where You Live

No two neighborhoods are exactly alike. Make a big deal out of what you've got that's unique

"There is no there *there*." This criticism, first voiced by writer Gertrude Stein about her hometown of Oakland, California is about the worst thing you can say about a place. Stein fled Oakland, California for Paris, never looking back, but her damning words have been repeated millions of times to dismiss seemingly dull cities, towns, and suburbs everywhere.

Stein was dead wrong. Every place has something to offer. But if you don't make an effort to show it off, you can't blame people, even those who live there, for thinking there is nothing of interest in your neighborhood.

The Local Distinctiveness Project, based in London, wants to stop the spread of bland uniformity around Britain and the world. It came out with a few questions for people to consider about their home turf: "What makes this place different from another? Which are the natural, man-made, and cultural elements that combine to tell you that you are in your place and not another community 2, 20, or 200 miles away? Are there local details and regional touchstones you can identify?"

To get started, the Local Distinctiveness Project urges you to organize people for a walk around the neighborhood. As you walk, gather ideas from what you see and who you talk to. The next step is a community workshop where everyone is free to contribute their ideas about what makes your place special. Then, "incorporate your findings on a ... map and put it up in a public place for all to see, discuss, and act upon."

It could be an ethnic flavor, like Japantown in San Jose, California the Finnish heritage of Thunder Bay, Ontario, Canada or the Brazilian immigrant communities around Boston. Residents of Saint-Boniface, the old French quarter of Winnipeg, Canada built a French-Canadian cultural center that has become a lively hub of community life in the area. Covington, Kentucky, across the river from Cincinnati, Ohio, drew on its German roots to revitalize its downtown district as "MainStrasse."

A neighborhood in Mason City, Iowa, showcases its many prairie-style homes. The Fan District in Richmond, Virginia, renewed itself through Victorian architecture, trumpeting the elegance and beauty of its old houses. Many cities from Chicago to Vancouver to L.A. now take pride in their "bungalow belts," although just a few years ago these small, turn-of-the-20th-century homes were considered outdated and a distinct liability. Meanwhile, older neighborhoods in Southern towns like Houston and New Orleans are preserving and promoting the classic shotgun houses built for working-class families. The Minneapolis suburb of Richfield brags about its well-preserved 1950s feel now that "mid-century" design is back in fashion.

It's not always so obvious what sets your community apart. It might be proximity to a college, a park, a religious institution, or a waterfront. Maybe it has an artsy or working-class identity. Perhaps there is a concentration of a certain type of business, such as vintage clothes shops, corner taverns, or hardware supply stores. Locally grown products have put Gilroy, California (garlic), and Vidalia, Georgia (what else? Sweet Vidalia onions), on the map. In San Antonio, Texas, the Mexican business district of Market Square advertises itself as the birthplace of the fajita.

Perhaps your neighborhood is special because of some annual event, like the San Gennaro Festival in New York's Little Italy or the Groundhog Day celebration in which Punxsutawney Phil steps into the spotlight in the Pennsylvania town of the same name. Look back into history to find something of interest. Northfield, Minnesota, commemorates a failed bank heist by Jesse James in a Main Street museum and annual celebration. Savannah heralds itself as the birthplace of the Girl Scouts, and Camden, Maine, erected a statue of poet and native daughter Edna St. Vincent Millay. The Plateau area of Montreal prides itself on being the home of poet and singer Leonard Cohen.

Your neighborhood's claim to fame may be more modest, but no less important in defining the soul of the community. It may

Every community has something that sets it apart from others — distinctive architecture, businesses, ethnic groups, history. In Greenwich Village, which is rich in Italian heritage, the Old World sport of bocce ball is popular.

be something as simple as an impressive collection of oak trees or the determined efforts of some local character, like the devout man who built "the world's smallest grotto" — a curious four-seat chapel fashioned out of concrete and old bottles — in his backyard in Iowa City.

As a neighborhood, you might decide to create something brand-new that expresses your community spirit. A bike trail or a public art project or a plaza commemorating something of importance to the community. The Local Distinctiveness Project suggests encouraging local shops to feature locally made products and printing up postcards "that capture the essence of your place," using the work of neighborhood photographers or artists.

The small city of Freiburg ranks as the number one place Germans say they would like to move to. Yet it doesn't have the cutting-edge energy of Berlin, the artistic sophistication of Munich, the historical splendor of Heidelberg, the economic clout of Frankfurt. What accounts for Freiburg's wide appeal as a place to live? A city council member explains that it's the residents' own pride in the place. Freiburgers have always relished the local cuisine, preferred the hearty local wines, ardently supported the local culture, and appreciated the scenic setting in the Black Forest. When Allied bombers leveled the center of town during World War II, it was rebuilt exactly as it had been — including the old-fashioned open gutters that allow rainfall to rush through downtown like a mountain stream on its way to the nearby Rhine River. The gutters have become one of the distinguishing traits of a very distinguished city.

RESOURCE

Local Distinctiveness Project: www.commonground.org.uk/ distinctiveness/d-index.html

The power of apple dumplings

Cambridge, Ontario, Canada

When the congregation at Wesley Church in Cambridge, Ontario, needed money to fix the roof, they came up with an enterprising solution: Sell apple dumplings with coffee and tea. They wisely decided to set up the new operation on Saturday mornings, coinciding with a weekly farmers market held next door to the church.

Soon, a group of 20 church volunteers calling themselves "The Apple Corps" started making dumplings from a favorite recipe. Now it's a community tradition for shoppers at the farmers market to stop inside the church for a hot apple dumpling doused in special sauce. The local newspaper, *Cambridge Now,* proclaimed that the dumplings tasted like a "sweet little piece of heaven"

and named the volunteer cooks "The Fellowship of the Dumpling" because "it is truly about fellowship and dumplings … and working together … and success."

The Apple Corps is a success not only because the volunteers have raised substantial money for the church (close to $50,000 in one year), but also because they have given the whole town a place and reason to gather every Saturday morning.

Wesley Church raises as much as $50,000 a year selling apple dumplings to towns-people in Cambridge, Ontario.

Build on What's Good to Make Things Better

It's just as important to understand what's going right in your neighborhood as it is to change what's going wrong

A public market in Porto Alegre, Brazil, is a key asset for the local community.

The biggest problem in many neighborhoods — especially low-income ones — is caused by perception more than reality. A part of town gets a reputation for being "bad," "tough," or "declining," and that reputation is constantly reinforced in the media and local gossip. A negative incident that happens in such a neighborhood is widely reported as more evidence of "social breakdown," whereas the same thing occurring in a different part of town is described as "an unfortunate event" and quickly forgotten.

Many well-intentioned efforts to help these afflicted areas wind up stigmatizing the community even more. They focus on everything that's wrong: bad schools, bad crime, bad housing, bad kids, and bad economic opportunities. In the end, even the people who live there start to feel hopeless about the place and powerless to do anything to change things. It's all just bad. Yet even in the most economically and socially challenged communities, there are a lot of good things going on that can be used as the building blocks to make improvements.

On paper, things looked bleak for the Grand Boulevard neighborhood in Chicago. More than 80 percent of the children in the area lived in poverty, and unemployment was 34 percent. Yet below the surface, not measured in government statistics or visible on a quick drive through its rundown streets, there were substantial reasons for optimism. This African-American community of 36,000 on the city's south side was home to no fewer than 320 citizens groups working to improve life in the neighborhood.

Grand Boulevard's residents were not just hapless victims waiting for someone from the outside to rescue them; they were taking matters into their own hands. The citizens groups — which ranged from church committees to senior citizens' centers to mothers' support groups — were mostly involved in basic caretaking, such as providing support for single mothers or taking in abandoned children. But after a number of these groups organized themselves into the Grand Boulevard Federation, they broadened their mission to creating jobs in the neighborhood and improving social services. They formed partnerships with government agencies, nonprofit organizations, and businesses, including United Parcel Service, which reserved 50 part-time jobs for Grand Boulevard residents needing to get on their feet. This has made a big difference for Grand Boulevard — in concrete economic and social measures, but also in bolstering the community's own faith that it can solve its problems.

"For the last 40 or 50 years [social planners] have been looking at communities in terms of their needs," says Jody Kretzmann, co-director of the Asset-Based Community Development Institute at Northwestern University. "We have run into a brick wall with that approach." Kretzmann and his colleague John McKnight of Northwestern have pioneered a new approach to urban problems that starts with looking at the assets that exist in a community, rather than just listing what's wrong. This empowers people, Kretzmann explains, drawing on the abilities and insight of local residents to solve a neighborhood's problems. But he is careful to note that this does not mean that troubled neighborhoods don't need outside help.

Any neighborhood can benefit from taking stock of its strengths. Kretzmann suggests that all local revitalization efforts begin with an assets inventory, which can be as simple as a brainstorming session on what's great about the neighborhood. Solicit the opinions of everyone, including youngsters and senior citizens, when compiling your list.

Jim Diers, a veteran activist who has held workshops throughout Seattle to help residents capitalize on the advantages of their neighborhoods, says that "the assets a neighborhood can build on range from natural features to a school playground, great stores, networks, organizations, artists, and the whole range of human and financial resources, energy, creativity, and ideas. Whether it's a restaurant with especially delicious food, a gigantic cedar tree, or a long-time resident, a neighborhood treasure is something that makes us glad we live where we do."

RESOURCES

Grand Boulevard neighborhood: "Asset management," www.pps.org

Jody Kretzmann and the Asset-Based Community Development Institute: www.northwestern.edu/ipr/a bcd.html

Building Communities from the Inside Out by John P. Kretzmann and John L. McKnight (Institute for Policy Research, 1993)

Jim Diers: home.comcast.net/~jimdiers

Neighborhood Power: Building Community the Seattle Way by Jim Diers (University of Washington Press, 2004)

Define the Boundaries of Your Neighborhood

It's hard to maintain a sense of community when you don't know where it starts or ends

People who cherish American cities often seem to fall in love with Pittsburgh, Pennsylvania. It certainly isn't the fanciest, richest, most sophisticated, or most glamorous town. Just the opposite. It wears its blue-collar, hard-working, Iron City image proudly. Indeed, local professor Richard Florida — who originated the "creative class" theory, which states that cities attracting the well-educated workers who drive today's economy will be the ones that thrive — long warned that Pittsburgh was falling behind on key indicators that measure a successful city. Florida himself eventually relocated to Washington, DC.

Yet Pittsburgh continually ranks high on lists of the best places in America to live. There's something about the place that nurtures fierce loyalty in local residents and excites the interest of outside observers. What is it? Several people point to its many lively and distinct neighborhoods. Because the city is dotted with steep hills and deep ravines, many areas are worlds unto themselves with only bridges or winding streets connecting them to the rest of town. This instills a strong sense of community identity and economic self-sufficiency. When it takes extra effort to get someplace else, you pay more attention to what happens in your own part of town.

East Liberty, a predominantly African-American neighborhood in the hills of Pittsburgh's East End, is singled out by Roberta Brandes Gratz, author of several books on urban revitalization, as a success story in the making. In 1950, East Liberty's business district was often called the third busiest in Pennsylvania after downtown Philadelphia and downtown Pittsburgh, but it became a tragic victim of the urban renewal plans of the 1960s. The neighborhood was ripped up to make way for destructive road projects that wiped out almost half the

Pittsburgh is celebrated for the distinctiveness and vitality of its neighborhoods, like Highland Park.

ALEX BELLOTI

community. East Liberty was also chosen as the site of not one, but three high-rise public-housing complexes.

Through the '60s, '70s, and '80s the community declined in part because of its physical isolation from more prosperous areas of Pittsburgh. Yet the isolation also fostered a strong sense of community, which began to bear fruit in the 1990s with citizen-led efforts to revive the neighborhood economy and undo damage done by the large-scale road and housing projects. Already, some of the streets have reverted back to their more hospitable pre-1960 configuration,

with more to follow. Two of the high-rise housing projects have been torn down, with the last one slated for demolition in a few years.

Even neighborhoods facing less-serious problems benefit from having well-defined boundaries. It's hard to instill any sense of community if you are not even sure what's in the neighborhood and what's not. Often, as in the case of East Liberty, it's obvious that a valley, waterway, railroad tracks, park or highway marks the border. But sometimes you must draw your own lines. If city government does not designate formal neighborhoods in your town, then citizens should get together to do it themselves by creating their own neighborhood organization. "As nearly as possible," architectural theorist Christopher Alexander advises, "use natural geographic and historical boundaries to mark these communities."

When it comes to neighborhoods, like so many human institutions, small is definitely beautiful. It's hard to foster a sense of community or get things done in an area that encompasses too much space or includes too many people. In his classic book, *A Pattern Language,* Alexander recommends that cities and towns be comprised of neighborhoods of "not more than 300 yards across with no more than 400 to 500 inhabitants ... Keep major roads outside these neighborhoods."

The city of Minneapolis, which has divided itself into 81 separate neighborhoods, each with an elected local board, has found success with slightly larger units averaging 4,000 to 5,000 people. But even here, experience has shown that things run less smoothly sometimes in the larger neighborhoods.

It's best that every neighborhood have an identifiable center, such as a shopping district, park, school, or library, to distinguish it. You will probably want to incorporate this center, or some other landmark, into the name of your neighborhood to let people know exactly

where it is. If there's a traditional name for your area — the South End, Goosetown, Fort Road, Little Manila, etc. — it makes sense to use that rather than inventing something new, which could cause confusion. But if the name your neighborhood now goes by is bureaucratic or dull, seriously consider changing it to something more descriptive. The whole point is to create an identity that people will identify with and feel proud about. Jones Addition (if no one remembers who Jones was) or the Mid-Sector Ward 14 probably doesn't do the job.

New Yorkers' sense of geography was forever changed in the '60s and '70s with the appearance of new neighborhood designations like the East Village, SoHo (South of Houston), and TriBeCa (Triangle Below Canal). San Francisco followed suit with SoMa (South of Market), Denver with LoDo (Lower Downtown), and many districts beginning with "So," "No," and "Lo" now flourish across the continent. In Brooklyn there's even DUMBO to delineate an up-and-coming neighborhood (Down Under the Manhattan Bridge Overpass). Besides adding a little fun to the city map, these names highlight where new bursts of energy and creativity are taking place.

The next step is to put up signs that let folks (including those who live there) know they're entering your neighborhood. Call on the talents of local artists to give them some flair. You might even consider a public art project to create neighborhood entrances that capture the area's personality. Classic examples, well worth imitating, are the colorful gateways in Chinatown districts from Victoria, BC, to Washington, DC that tell folks, in dazzling red and gold colors, exactly where they are.

RESOURCES

East Liberty Development Inc.: www.eastliberty.org

Roberta Brandes Gratz: www.robertabrandesgratz.com

Cities Back from the Edge by Roberta Brandes Gratz with Norman Mintz (John Wiley, 1998)

The Living City by Roberta Brandes Gratz (John Wiley, 1994)

A Pattern Language by Christopher Alexander (Oxford University Press, 1977)

Root, Root, Root for the Home Team

If we don't get involved in local athletics, it's a shame. We'll miss a lot of excitement

Big-time sports have become a sorry spectacle with rampant steroid and drug use; greedy, unsportsmanlike owners; greedy, overpaid players; recruiting and pay-off scandals at colleges; thuggish behavior by athletes off the field; coaches who would do anything to win; and sports-writers and broadcasters who don't understand it's only a game. It's enough to make you vow never to set foot inside a stadium, arena, or ballpark again.

But don't despair. There are still games being played that feature honorable coaches and talented players who play for fun, not fame or money. Actually, they're going on right in your community. Stroll down to the Little League diamond, the local high school gym, or the bowling alley.

Your neighbors may not be as accomplished as NFL stars or World Cup soccer champions, but they put their hearts into it just the same. The games are just as exciting, and you can personally congratulate the winners afterwards. Maybe buy them milk shakes or beer at the local hangout.

Or become part of the games yourself. From tennis to horseshoes, opportunities abound to join a team, league, or tournament. Contact the parks board or consult the sports page to see what's going on. Even if you don't feel up to running 800 meters or lacing up hockey skates, there are plenty of other ways to join in the fun as a coach, team sponsor, referee, fundraiser, refreshment stand manager, scorekeeper, or advocate for local sports in your community.

Bemidji, Minnesota, has become world famous for its curling champions. Though the city's population is only 12,000, local teams won the opportunity to represent the United States in both women's and men's competitions at the 2005 World Curling Championship. Bemidji also fielded members for both the men's and women's US Olympic curling teams for 2006,

Ready. Set. Go! A track event in Winter Park, Florida, welcomes runners of every age.

including Pete Fenson, skip (captain) of the bronze medal winning men's team. The skip of the women's team, Cassie Johnson, was also from Bemidji. Both Olympic teams did their training at the Bemidji Curling Club.

The Curling Club is a focal point of the community, offering men's, women's, mixed, and numerous junior leagues. According to its website, "some leagues are very social, some are competitive, but most are a good mix in between." Even if you've never played the sport, club manager Bob Fenson, father of Olympic star Pete, will be glad to help you get started.

You could do the same for your town or neighborhood in ultimate Frisbee, croquet, aikido, steeplechase, Ping-Pong, or tug-of-war. All it usually takes is one or two dedicated individuals to organize a league, inspire potential players, and lobby civic officials for the proper facilities so that local talents can develop their potential.

In 1978, Indianapolis embarked on an ambitious campaign to become the amateur sports capital of the world. The idea was to boost the city's image as a dull place and address some of its economic problems. Part of the strategy was to bring major amateur sports events to town as an economic development tool, but there was also an emphasis on promoting local youth programs, which has paid off. Indianapolis enjoys a considerably improved image today as national media frequently mention its emphasis on sports.

Undertaking a similar initiative in your town or neighborhood might yield not only community pride but also social progress. When Minneapolis was experiencing an unprecedented upturn in youth crime and gang activity a few years ago, Mayor Sharon Sayles Belton responded with the "Midnight Basketball" program, which kept gymnasiums and community centers open late at night so kids would have somewhere to go where they could stay out of trouble. The crime and gang problems soon declined. When recent cuts in federal and state aid to the city forced reductions in the program, crime problems rose again.

RESOURCE

Bemidji Curling Club:
 www.bemidjicurling.org

Celebrate Your Place in the World

Capture your neighborhood's spirit in song, print, paint, or even T-shirts

Nearly every tourist in Paris makes a pilgrimage to Montmartre. It's difficult to reach, up a steep hill, and quite plain compared to the grand boulevards and great landmarks for which the city is famous. Yet visitors come by the thousands each day to wander its few small streets, snap photos, and sip an espresso in the cafés. Why? Because they've seen it in famous paintings, and now they want to see it in real life.

Montmartre was Paris' artistic center in the late 19th century, a low-rent haven that was home or hangout to many of the great Impressionist and Post-Impressionist painters. These artists, of course, painted their surroundings, and now the whole world has a definite picture of this out-of-the-way neighborhood in its mind.

It's interesting to explore how your place in the world has been depicted by artists, writers, filmmakers, or musicians through the years. Unlike Paris, however, it may be old postcards and pamphlets that capture the spirit of your neighborhood rather than Renoir and Victor Hugo. Try the library, historical society, local museums, and the shelves of used bookstores, record shops, galleries, and antique shops in the vicinity.

It's even more fun to capture the essence of your home turf in a short story, blog, song, cartoon, photographs, stand-up comedy routine, computer game, or whatever medium you most like to use to express yourself. Tell the neighborhood's favorite stories, describe the local characters, offer a vivid portrait of what everyday life is like.

Maybe you'll make your community a little bit famous, like the Greek neighborhoods of Chicago in *My Big Fat Greek Wedding* or "Luckenbach, Texas" in the classic country song by Waylon Jennings. Perhaps local officials will honor your work, as they did author Beverly Cleary's. A park in northeast Portland, Oregon features statues of her beloved characters Ramona, Henry, Beezus, and Ribsy, who roamed through nearby streets in Cleary's still widely read novels for young readers. Jack Kerouac, chronicler of the Beat generation in the 1950s, has an alley named for him that runs between two of his favorite San Francisco hangouts: the City Lights bookstore and Vesuvio's Bar. He is one of many artistic figures honored in a city that is frequently the setting for books and films.

Most likely you'll simply have the satisfaction of giving your neighbors a moment of pleasure and pride when they see your work hanging in the corner coffee shop, printed in the local newspaper, or presented at the community center. Most of us live in the kinds of places that never appear on TV shows or in magazine articles, not to mention poems and paintings. That can sometimes make us feel our lives don't matter much, especially compared to

These kids might make their hometown famous when they grow up to become great artists.

the glamorous folks in Manhattan or Malibu, who we see depicted all the time in movies and novels and on TV. It's empowering to see that the places we know are also worthy of creative exploration.

This can be done with something as simple as a t-shirt. Think of the many times you've seen people advertising famous spots like "Las Vegas" or "Aspen" on their chests. Why not do the same for your neck of the woods? Print up shirts, tote bags, or bumper stickers celebrating your neighborhood.

And when someone asks about Sweet Auburn, San Pedro, Westminster, Willy Street, Royal Oak, or Hardwick, tell them it's a great place. (They are, respectively, Atlanta's historic African-American hub; Los Angeles's port; a leafy corner of Winnipeg; the near east side of Madison, Wisconsin; a suburb next door to Detroit; and a lively town in northeast Vermont)

The little bus station that could

Corpus Christi, Texas

The phrase "bus transfer center" may not conjure images of an exciting public place. Most of these stations are sterile, soulless facilities designed for the convenience of buses rather than riders. But not in Corpus Christi, Texas, where the local arts council worked with community residents to create 1,500 handmade tiles to imbue their new bus transfer center with an appealing community identity. The tiles were used to decorate benches and walls at the station. Everyone from the mayor to local schoolchildren to inmates at a nearby jail designed tiles.

This art project helped achieve the larger goal of creating a transit station that also functioned as a community destination. Since downtown Corpus Christi lacked real gathering places, the regional transit authority wanted to both attract riders and create a place for people to go. The Staples Street Station, designed by architect John Wright based on conceptual plans that came out of a series of public meetings, has become a bustling spot visited by 5,000 bus riders and others every day.

The handmade tiles symbolize how the station arose from the efforts of the local community, giving people a sense of ownership of their transit system. In recognition of the station's success, the project team received a presidential design award.

RESOURCE

Staples Street bus station: www.pps.org/info/aboutpps/greatest_hits_4

Local folks in Corpus Christi, Texas, designed tiles that grace their stylish and lively bus transfer station.

GEOFF CARTER

A warm welcome

Laguna Beach, California

For years, a town greeter welcomed everyone to downtown Laguna Beach, California. His wide smile and friendly "hello" made a great first impression on visitors and lifted the spirits of locals. The original town greeter was a gregarious Danish immigrant named Eiler Larsen, who could be found at the corner of the Pacific Coast Highway and Forest Avenue in downtown Laguna Beach, calling out, "Hello there!" in a booming voice to everyone who passed by on foot or in a car. Sporting hair down past his shoulders and a great, grey beard, Larsen would happily offer directions, practical advice, and pearls of wisdom to anyone who asked. People who grew up in Laguna Beach during the '50s and '60s still remember him warmly as a steadfast, reassuring presence.

Although Larsen was recognized by the city council as the Official Greeter of Laguna Beach, the "town greeter" position was always informal — a personal calling that Larsen chose to pursue when he was not working as a gardener. After he died in 1975, he was memorialized with two statues at local establishments. The greeter tradition was carried on by a series of successors. Sometimes several years passed without a greeter before someone felt inspired to take over the role. While there is no one occupying the spot on Forest Avenue right now, a new volunteer may step forward at any time to offer a friendly welcome to everyone who passes by.

A statue honors the town greeter, Eiler Larsen, who once welcomed visitors and locals alike to downtown Laguna Beach, California.

Chapter 8
Getting Things Done

How to make your dreams a reality

 Dare to dream

 Work with city hall

 Have some fun

 Forget city hall

 Never underestimate the power of a meal

 Take over from city hall

 Fight city hall

 Do nothing in particular

Dare to Dream

Drawing on your imagination is the first step to reviving your neighborhood

Fixing up a neighborhood, especially an economically disadvantaged one, is hard work. It takes lots of planning, energy, and determination. You're attending, and in some cases organizing, many public meetings. You've got to excite skeptical neighbors and win over even more skeptical politicians, developers, and funders. Such an undertaking calls for level-headed, realistic, practical, no-nonsense thinking. But if that's all you give it, you're missing a huge opportunity.

Transforming your neighborhood into a place that people are proud to call home depends on inspiration as well as perspiration.

From the southeast side of Seattle comes uplifting evidence of the important roles that a vivid sense of imagination and a clear community vision play in improving neighborhood life. The Columbia City district was founded in the 1890s as a commuter suburb and was later absorbed into fast-growing Seattle. Although run-down, the neighborhood had a distinctive historic character that aided community-led efforts to revitalize the area in the 1990s. But one half-block stretch of Columbia City's downtown proved stubbornly resistant to change. Even as substantial

Teens on the Upper West Side of New York envisioned a skate park as part of a class project. Then they made it happen.

PETER DOLLE

improvements were being made throughout this working-class and ethnic community, merchants could not be persuaded to open businesses in these particular buildings. The shop windows remained boarded up, giving the neighborhood a blighted look despite all the progress.

"The buildings had been empty for 20 years," notes Jim Diers, a local resident who at the time headed Seattle's Department of Neighborhoods. Finally, at one local meeting, "someone suggested that if the community couldn't attract real businesses, they could at least pretend," Diers recounts in his compelling book *Neighbor Power.*

And that's exactly what Columbia City residents did. Working with artists from the Southeast Seattle Arts Council, they painted the community's dreams on the plywood covering the windows: an ice-cream parlor, a toy store, a dance studio, a bookshop, and a hat shop.

"The murals looked so realistic that passing motorists sometimes stopped to shop," Diers writes. "The murals also captured the imagination of a developer and several business owners. Within a year, every one of the murals had to be removed because real businesses wanted to locate there."

Columbia City saw its dreams come true when a new Italian deli, a brewpub, and a cooperative art gallery opened in the abandoned block. The gallery actually grew out of a town meeting where local residents offered visions for the neighborhood.

RESOURCES

Columbia City:
   www.raniervalley.org
Jim Diers:
   home.comcast.net/~jimdiers/
Neighbor Power: Building Community the Seattle Way by Jim Diers (University of Washington Press, 2004)

Have Some Fun

Community projects that succeed are the ones in which people have a good time. Make sure to plan some parties, parades, and games

The task of improving your neighborhood often feels overwhelming. What needs to be done? How do you do it? Where do you start? Many seasoned activists agree that the best way to get things going is to play around. When a community project is enjoyable and entertaining, it stands a much better chance of being successful.

Having a good time is not just an afterthought. Planning some fun as part of every meeting or event is a winning strategy. After a visioning session, clear chairs and tables for a dance party. Rendezvous for dessert at someone's house when a public hearing is over. Celebrate progress toward your goals with a homemade parade or ice-cream social.

In Monterey, California, Quinton Roland of Hometown Economics and Development has invented a kind of board game to help people imagine new possibilities for their neighborhoods. Citizens come together and have a ball using small wooden blocks to literally reconstruct their neighborhood in miniature scale. These Q-Blox, as they're called, can be arranged to resemble schools, churches, trees, houses of different styles, parks, apartment buildings, sidewalks, town homes, fountains, parking garages, landscaping, storefronts, etc.

Q-Blox offers citizens a good look at what proposed developments in their area would actually mean and a sense of how their own ideas would look if they were built. It's an engaging way for people to explore and dream together about the future of their community. It's also a very practical tool for making critical decisions. As Roland notes, "When finished up with a particular Q-Blox configuration, one can quickly tally up the square footage of commercial and public space as well as the number of jobs created, housing units, and parking stalls."

RESOURCE
Q-Blox:
www.vibranthometown.com

Rule number one for improving your community: Keep a sense of humor.

Before the construction of the NoHo Transit Arts Park ...

A star is born in North Hollywood

Los Angeles, California

The Los Angeles Neighborhood Initiative (LANI) is a nonprofit organization dedicated to boosting community-driven revitalization and transit access in low-income Los Angeles neighborhoods. The services that LANI provides to communities are catalysts for something much bigger. Each time it helps a community revitalize a transportation corridor, the project attracts additional resources and economic activity to the area.

One particular project, the North Hollywood (NoHo) Transit Arts District, went above and beyond expectations. The transportation "corridor" consisted of a vacant lot; two vacant storefronts; poorly maintained businesses, sidewalks, and streetscapes; and a single pole to mark the location of the bus stop.

The community came together to discuss its vision for the bus stop, and residents decided they wanted more than a bus stop — they wanted a public space. The group began looking for street vendors — a coffee cart, a breakfast vendor, etc. — to set up shop on the sidewalk next to the bus stop in order to attract more people to the area. Instead, they received interest from a restaurateur who wanted to locate in the adjacent vacant storefront. The restaurateur also agreed to put a sidewalk café in the vacant lot.

The initial success of the restaurant and café sparked additional improvements to the area: businesses filled nearby vacant storefronts, landscaping was done along the sidewalks, murals were painted to bring blank, sterile walls to life. The project proved a catalyst for something more — it created 30 new jobs and stimulated an additional $600,000 investment

The Los Angeles Neighborhood Initiative transformed a forlorn bus stop into a lively community hub.

... and after, a pleasant place for the community.

.in property improvements. Through the hard work of community stakeholders, in partnership with LANI and the LA Municipal Community Redevelopment Agency, NoHo has been transformed from a dreary thoroughfare to a burgeoning district with coffee shops, restaurants, and eclectic retail.

RESOURCE

Los Angeles Neighborhood
Initiative: www.lani.org

The fondest moments in everyone's lives often happen over a table full of food.

Never Underestimate the Power of a Meal

A pot of chili, hamburgers on the grill, or a platter of pasta can revolutionize your neighborhood

Anthropologist Margaret Mead was absolutely right when she declared, "Never doubt that a small group of thoughtful, committed citizens can change the world. Indeed, it is the only thing that ever has."

A few years back, residents of the Kingfield and East Harriet neighborhoods of Minneapolis proved Mead right once again when they successfully rose up against plans to widen a street running through the heart of their community.

A group that met for potlucks sparked a chain reaction across town as neighborhood after neighborhood began to stand up to auto-cratic road plans. Until that point, city engineers had the power to widen any street they wanted, no matter how much community opposition there was. But now traffic-calming projects are sprouting across the city, and cars no longer rule the road the way they once did.

The origins of this protest can be traced back to a small group of neighbors who began sharing potluck dinners on Friday nights. The talk at these events often turned to issues facing the neighborhood, so when someone brought up the pending plans to widen Lyndale Avenue, the group sprang into action. The neighbors drafted a flyer explaining why the project was a terrible idea and then fanned out to every house within three blocks of the avenue, tucking flyers under doors. Jacquelynn Goessling, one of the organizers, remembers, "We basically just outlined the cost that neighborhood residents would pay in terms of safety, property values, noise, and peace of mind. The people at the meeting understood what was at stake …. And to think it all began with people eating salad, nibbling on cheese, and drinking wine together."

Without the potluck dinners, the group could never have moved into action so quickly to get a message out to the whole neighborhood. The road widening would probably have been a done deal before anyone raised objections to it. These people had come together for purely social reasons, but they evolved into an effective neighborhood lobbying force. To celebrate the victory, they took the idea of potluck one step further by throwing a "We Saved Lyndale" street dance for people from every neighborhood along the avenue.

Sometimes the impact of bringing people to the table for a meal is less dramatic but no less meaningful. Springfield, Massachusetts, trumpets its community spirit each year by throwing the world's largest pancake breakfast. Everyone sits down at one enormous table and digs into a hearty breakfast. In 2005, proud Springfielders gobbled down countless pancakes accompanied by 450 gallons of maple syrup and 2.3 tons of butter.

Lambertville, New Jersey, drew upon the same community spirit when it held the Great American Spaghetti Supper to mark the town's 150th birthday. Most of the town turned out — despite threatening gray skies — for a festive, never-to-be-forgotten dinner. A big storm finally blew in as dessert was being served, but as Gabrielle Hamilton, daughter of the man who conceived the idea, wrote in *Saveur* magazine, that didn't dampen the high spirits. "The party continues down side streets, on porches, and under eaves, old timers crouched next to newcomers. We drink the last of the red wine in the rain, eating soggy cake, reveling in our community."

Any time neighbors sit down to a meal together, it makes a difference. It doesn't have to be a huge feast or even a home-cooked dinner — a couple of pepperoni pizzas from the place around the corner will do. What's important are the connections that are made. They could lead to a community uprising, a good friendship, or just a closer sense of cooperation. And that's what life is all about.

RESOURCE

Springfield Pancake Breakfast: www.spiritofspringfield.org

Fight City Hall

Yes! You can ... and you can win

The old adage that you can't fight city hall is proven wrong almost every day as citizens across the continent stand up to challenge municipal officials on a wide array of issues. It was once easy for city officials to simply shrug off people's concerns, but since the 1960s — when neighborhood movements in many cities stopped unpopular new freeways and urban renewal projects — public officials have been more cautious about disregarding the wishes of their constituents. An organized force of citizens that is not afraid to challenge the status quo in city hall can bring about significant change in its community.

Lyndale Avenue was already notorious for its speeding traffic, which ran past homes and small businesses on the south side of Minneapolis, when the city unveiled plans to widen the street. A group of people (see "Never Underestimate the Power of a Meal," see page 158) living near the street called their newly elected city council member and asked her to help them stop the project, but the council member declined to take a stand. This spurred the group to organize neighborhood opposition to the project, which resulted in more than 400 angry neighbors packing a public meeting at a local community center. When the floor was opened up to questions from the audience, a realtor stood up and offered statistics describing the steep decline in property values residents on Lyndale and surrounding streets would see. Next up was the principal of a Catholic elementary school on the avenue, who predicted, "If this street is widened, we will see kids being run over and killed." It went on like that for several hours until the council member stood up to announce, there would be no widening the street.

RESOURCE
Lyndale Avenue:
   www.lyndale.org

Suhair Lauck, owner of the Little Tea House, speaks up against street-widening in Memphis, Tennessee.

Spreading art all over town

Zurich, Switzerland

It's widely acknowledged that benches are good places to sit, but few people realize they also make great springboards for art. In the summer of 2001, people in Zurich, Switzerland, discovered how much a little imagination could transform their city when more than 1,000 artist-designed benches were installed all over town. The benches were painted, decorated, or sculpted to evoke everything from an alpine lake to abstract expressions to a cook flirting with a waitress.

Organized by City Vereinigung Zurich (Zurich Town Center Association), an association of local businesses dedicated to creating a more livable city center, the exhibit allowed iindividuals and organizations to sponsor the artist of their choice to design a bench. The only restriction was that the benches could not be used for advertising or political topics.

Many other cities have programs where local artists are matched with businesses to create public art projects, but from a placemaking perspective, few have been as successful as the Zurich benches. Not only were the benches easy-to-use amenities, there was such a great variety that people could choose benches that best suited their personality. It almost seemed that some bench sitters had been conceived by the artists as part of their work.

Artists designed public benches in Zurich, Switzerland, that attract all sorts of admirers.

Work with City Hall

Good government depends on the participation of citizens — so what are you waiting for?

Too often, government seems out of touch with the people it is supposed to serve. Congress, the White House, state and provincial legislatures, governors' mansions, Parliament, and the prime minister's office seem remote from our lives and largely indifferent to what happens in our communities. But local government is another story. City council members, mayors, and heads of municipal departments live in the same place we do. They are not insulated from the problems that pop up around town, and they can't afford to be indifferent to opportunities that arise.

Look to Charleston, South Carolina, for one of the best examples of what a local leader can accomplish. Joe Riley is more than Charleston's mayor. He's a good neighbor, greeting everyone on the street as he walks downtown and genuinely listening when citizens talk about what's going on in the community. Riley watches over local streets and parks like a proud homeowner, looking for what's working well and what needs improvement. During 30 years in office, Riley's careful attention to the details has helped Charleston make great strides to improve race relations, promote economic prosperity, reduce crime, and become a better place to live.

Every city, suburb, and town deserves public leaders like Joe Riley. But great leaders depend on dedicated citizens. You can help local officials do their best by respectfully but firmly drawing their attention to what's going wrong around the community and pointing out opportunities to make things better. If politicians don't seem willing to listen, or if they prove unable to take necessary actions to make a difference, remember that the next time election season rolls around.

Local politics is a face-to-face affair. Candidates show up everywhere — at parades, ethnic festivals, county fairs, pancake breakfasts, and countless community meetings. The more

Neighborhood advocates seeking better parks worked with Baltimore's mayor to create a temporary town square in front of city hall to draw attention to the issue.

hands they shake and the more questions from voters they answer, the better their chances on election day. Take advantage of this accessibility by attending campaign events to raise the issues that most affect your community.

Sponsoring a candidates' forum or debate can be even more effective. Work with your neighborhood organization or community group and invite all the electoral hopefuls to answer questions from citizens at a local library or church hall. Bringing out a sizable, lively crowd is a surefire way to get politicians to take your concerns seriously.

As a community activist in low-income Seattle neighborhoods, Jim Diers expected a lot from local public officials. When they disappointed him, he wasn't shy about expressing his feelings. He once let a live chicken loose in the mayor's office to make a dramatic point about the city backing out of a commitment it had made on affordable housing issues. Diers worked indefatigably to excite people about Seattle's potential to be a great city for everyone living there. That's why former mayor Charles Royer — overlooking the incident with the chicken — appointed him director of the city's new Department of Neighborhoods in 1988.

The department was a bold experiment that explored how city government could respond more effectively to neighborhood issues. For the next 13 years, Diers and the citizens of Seattle pioneered a new vision of local governance that put neighborhood needs on the same level as economic development, streets, finances, and other municipal business. Diers, his staff, and the citizens they worked with have played a key role in building Seattle's global reputation as a livable city.

RESOURCES

City of Charleston mayor's office: www.ci.charleston.sc.us

Seattle Department of Neighborhoods: www.ci.seattle.wa.us/ neighborhoods/

Neighbor Power: Building Community the Seattle Way by Jim Diers (University of Washington Press, 2004)

Forget City Hall

Sometimes it's wiser to not ask permission from the authorities. Act first and wait for them to react

Traffic calming has swept the world over the past 15 years. It's based on the simple idea that cars and trucks don't have exclusive ownership of our streets. Streets are shared public space that also belongs to people on foot and bicycles, in baby strollers and wheelchairs. Traffic calming uses design features such as narrowed roads or elevated crosswalks to slow traffic and to assert pedestrians' inalienable right to cross the street.

This idea has altered the landscape of urban life in the Netherlands, Scandinavia, Germany, and Australia as people can now move about cities with more ease and pleasure. And now traffic calming is starting to make an impact in other parts of the world.

The origins of this ingenious idea can be traced to Delft, Netherlands, where residents of one neighborhood were fed up with cars racing along their streets, endangering children, pets, and peace of mind. One evening they decided to do something about it by dragging old couches and other furniture out into the roadway. They positioned these objects in such a way that cars could pass, but only if they slowed down. The police soon arrived on the scene and had to admit that this project, although clearly illegal, was a good idea. Soon the city itself was implementing similar plans of its own, called *woonerfs* (Dutch for "living yards"), on streets plagued by unruly motorists.

One can only imagine the response of politicians and engineers if these neighbors had meekly come to city hall to ask permission to partially block the streets. They would have been hooted right out of the building. By taking direct action, however, they saved their neighborhood and brought comfort and civility to cities around the world.

People in the Netherlands don't seek permission to take over part of the street for pedestrian uses. They just do it.

Design darts hit the bullseye

New York's Lower East Side

In New York's Lower East Side neighborhood, where Cantonese and Spanish are the languages most commonly spoken, communication issues pose unique challenges to community-based design efforts. But two high school interns at the Hester Street Collaborative — a small nonprofit that works with students and community members to improve public spaces — came up with an ingenious way to overcome the problem. They introduced the use of darts, stickers, and other nonverbal devices to help draft plans to improve a neighborhood.

The Design Darts work this way: Participants receive a batch of stickers they can use to mark elements of the neighborhood that don't meet the needs and desires of the community. Participants also receive diagrams showing various suggestions for improving the design of a place, such as an intersection or playground. The participants go out to the selected place and put the stickers where they believe the improvements should be applied. Volunteers take photographs to document the spots covered with the most stickers, and then the stickers are removed. The stickered spots are where the community starts its work.

The Hester Street Collaborative launched Design Darts with grade-school students and teachers at Public School 134 as part of an effort to improve a nearby community garden. To kick off the project, the students put stickers on areas of the garden that they wanted to improve. "The kids really enjoyed it," says Anne Frederick of the Collaborative. "The exercise raised the students' interest in the garden, and several joined a group of stakeholders who tend to the garden's continuing maintenance."

RESOURCE

Hester Street Collaborative:
www.hesterstreet.org

Students participate at a community meeting in New York's Lower East Side, using stickers to express their opinions on a prospective plan.

Bringing history back to life

Denver, Colorado

When urban renewal schemes tore through cities across America in the 1960s, historic districts everywhere succumbed to wrecking balls. Thanks to the passionate commitment of a few individuals, Denver's lower downtown (known as LoDo for short) escaped such a fate. To counter plans to demolish historic properties along Larimer Street, Dana and John Crawford led a group of investors who quietly bought a block of properties with special historic and architectural significance. Dana Crawford's research had revealed that one of the buildings on the block was the site of Denver's first log cabin, built by city founder General William Larimer.

"I felt this block — so important to the foundation of an entire community — absolutely had to be saved," says Crawford. The plan was to rehabilitate the buildings to attract restaurants, shops, galleries, and offices, but the pursuit of this dream meant a prolonged fight with Denver's Urban Renewal Authority and an intense search for financial backers. Both battles were ultimately won. Crawford persuaded local banks and the New York Life Insurance Company to help fund the undertaking, and the result was the re-use of historic properties and the creation of Larimer Square. The area became Denver's first historic district, emerging as a beacon of hope for downtowns across America.

Crawford invested 22 years of her life in Larimer Square and went on to preserve and adapt many more buildings throughout the downtown. Today, Larimer Square continues to set the pace as downtown's liveliest commercial district. It is proof that preserving a city's history can be much healthier for economic development and social progress than ill-advised "renewal" projects.

RESOURCE

LoDo District, Inc.:
    www.lodo.org

Now beloved by everybody in town, Denver's LoDo district once was targeted for the wrecking ball.

Take Over from City Hall

Successful programs in Brazil and Minnesota show how citizens can directly run their cities

One of the chief causes of cynicism about government is the feeling that citizens have no involvement in the political process, especially in decisions about how their money is spent. Even on the local level, the municipal budget is decided by politicians, while we pick up the tab. We have no say in what gets funded and what doesn't.

If elected officials encouraged a greater spirit of participation, it would not only enhance the reputation of politics, but would also increase the effectiveness of government. Citizens are the best authorities on what works and what doesn't work in their own communities. Taking advantage of their expertise to decide which programs deserve funding, and tapping their ideas to determine what else needs to be done can be invaluable in running a city. Two cities at opposite ends of the hemisphere have proven this works — and that it might make sense in your own town.

In Brazil, the city of Porto Alegre decided to draw on citizens' expertise after the Workers' Party was elected to office in 1989. The party threw open the budgeting process to anyone who wanted to take part. Citizens in this city of 1.3 million gathered in neighborhood assemblies to discuss what was most needed in their own parts of town and then elected representatives to advise the city council on financial priorities. This "participatory budget" process has been credited with

lowering unemployment, improving public transit, and revitalizing poor neighborhoods. The United Nations has identified Porto Alegre as the city with the best quality of life in Brazil.

Citizens in Minneapolis directly determine how some of their municipal tax money is spent by taking part in a unique program that allocates millions of dollars over a period of twenty years. Neighborhood activists across the city used to complain about the amount of municipal funding that went into downtown projects, while neighborhoods struggled with crime, housing, and economic issues. Former mayor Don Fraser and former deputy mayor Rip Rapson saw the legitimacy of these concerns and in 1991 responded with an inspired idea. They allowed neighborhoods decide how to spend $20 million a year, using money from property tax revenues coming out of taxpayer-supported downtown projects. That's how the innovative Neighborhood Revitalization Program (NRP) was born.

The city is divided into 81 neighborhoods, and each was allotted a certain sum of money based on its economic needs. Seventy-nine of these communities came together in a series of meetings to discuss what could be done to improve life in their part of town. Half of the NRP money was earmarked for housing programs, based on individual neighborhoods' own assessment of their needs and ideas for solutions. The rest of

the money was available for any project the neighborhood decided. Plans were carried out by a committee elected by residents, which worked with city staff.

The NRP unleashed a tide of remarkable creativity as Minneapolis residents conceived projects and innovations that had never before been discussed inside city hall. One community launched its own neighborhood school — a controversial idea at the time that has now become the norm throughout Minneapolis. Others refurbished business districts and established arts and community centers. Parks, trails, and libraries were improved. Many neighborhoods installed pedestrian-scaled lighting for their sidewalks. Politicians and city staff had previously rejected this idea, believing it was not important, but NRP showed just how strongly people wanted the lights in order to increase safety, encourage walking, and bring

some old-fashioned charm back to their streets. The NRP, which is still underway in a scaled-down form, literally changed the face of Minneapolis.

NRP has had a great impact on the city in other ways. The program inspired a new spirit of possibility throughout Minneapolis, especially in poorer areas, where people relished the chance to make decisions that affected their future. It helped citizens reengage with local government and offered an entry point for new civic leaders, some of whom now work in city hall themselves.

RESOURCE

Minneapolis Neighborhood
    Revitalization Program:
    www.nrp.org

Once in a while you need to remind politicians and city bureaucrats that they work for you.

Do Nothing in Particular

Sometimes it's important to simply enjoy what's already there

"I arise in the morning torn between a desire to improve (or save) the world and a desire to enjoy (or savor) the world," wrote the great American essayist E.B. White. "This makes it hard to plan the day."

Ah, that's the dilemma. You live in a nice place. But it could be nicer — if only the park were fixed up or the traffic slowed down, if the schools were better or the business district brighter.

So what to do first? You'd like to plop down on a bench for a while, soak up the sunshine, listen to the birds sing and the kids play, or just watch the world go by. But you really ought to be organizing a meeting, handing out flyers, and enlisting volunteers for the big fundraiser.

Actually, it's important to do both. Without taking time to truly savor your neighborhood, you lose touch with why you

The most effective community activists are those who regularly revel in the pleasures of their neighborhood.

love it in the first place. Soon, all you see is what's wrong. And that quickly diminishes your effectiveness as a community advocate. No one is inspired by harried, humorless leaders who would really rather be doing something else.

On a strategic as well as a personal level it's smart to take a long stroll every evening, linger at the sidewalk café, stop for a chat with neighbors, and just generally revel in all the great things your community offers. Otherwise, what's the point of living there?

In the Irish Hill neighborhood of Louisville, Kentucky, the Professional Porch Sitters union is coming to order. Crow Hollister, who founded the union, explains in *Orion* magazine that the organization attracts hard-working activists, professionals, artists, mothers, revolutionaries, and gardeners. "People like you," he says. "They work hard, volunteer in their community, sit on boards, have schedules to keep and chores that need tending." An agenda is dutifully handed out for each meeting, but there is nothing written on it. Iced tea is served, followed by beer. Stories begin to flow. Andy describes how his neighbor was visited by the windshield wiper fairy. Hillary talks about an article coming up in her self-published e-zine *Bejeezus*. Mike has the inside scoop on how to get the slabs of concrete they use on public benches for free. Then, Hollister dutifully reports, "a neighbor walking her dog is enticed to join us. A lot is getting accomplished."

The Professional Porch Sitters Union began on Crow Hollister's comfy front porch in 1999 and now features chapters across the country. Hollister encourages you to start your own, keeping in mind that the organization is governed by only one rule: "Sit down a spell. That can wait." He'd like to hear how it goes, but don't sweat it if you don't get around to writing him.

RESOURCES

Bejeezus e-zine:
  www.bejeezuszine.com
Orion Grassroots Network:
  "Professional Porch Sitters"
  www.orionsociety.org

About the Author

Jay Walljasper is Senior Fellow at Project for Public Spaces and Executive Editor of *Ode* magazine. His writing on community issues has appeared in many publications, including *The Nation, Preservation, The New Statesman,* and *Utne Reader,* where he was the Editor for many years. Walljasper is co-author (with Jon Spryde) of *Visionaries: People & Ideas to Change Your Life.* (New Society Publishers, 2001). Walljasper lives with his family in the Kingfield neighborhood of Minneapolis.

For more information please visit www.jaywalljasper.com.

About Project for Public Spaces

Project for Public Spaces Inc. is an internationally recognized non-profit that applies a community-based approach to the revitalization of neighborhoods and cities — an approach called "Placemaking."

Placemaking involves working with communities to develop public spaces that are well-used and safe, and that become catalysts for boosting the economic and social vitality of the community as a whole.

Since its founding in 1975, PPS has provided technical assistance, research, education, planning and design services to nearly 2,000 communities in 26 countries to help citizens create vibrant public places.

Forthcoming PPS publications will cover the following topics: how communities have created successful public markets; how to transform transit corridors into vital urban villages; and a practical guide to best research on public spaces.

For more information, please visit www.pps.org

Other books by Project for Public Spaces:

How to Turn a Place Around: A Handbook for Creating Successful Public Spaces

Public Markets and Community Revitalization

Public Parks, Private Partners

If you have enjoyed *The Great Neighborhood Book*
you might also enjoy other

BOOKS TO BUILD A NEW SOCIETY

Our books provide positive solutions for people who want to
make a difference. We specialize in:

**Environment and Justice • Conscientious Commerce
Sustainable Living • Ecological Design and Planning
Natural Building & Appropriate Technology • New Forestry
Educational and Parenting Resources • Nonviolence
Progressive Leadership • Resistance and Community**

New Society Publishers

ENVIRONMENTAL BENEFITS STATEMENT

New Society Publishers has chosen to produce this book on Enviro 100, recycled paper made with **100% post consumer waste**, processed chlorine free, and old growth free.

For every 5,000 books printed, New Society saves the following resources:[1]

27	Trees
2,404	Pounds of Solid Waste
2,645	Gallons of Water
3,450	Kilowatt Hours of Electricity
4,370	Pounds of Greenhouse Gases
19	Pounds of HAPs, VOCs, and AOX Combined
7	Cubic Yards of Landfill Space

[1]Environmental benefits are calculated based on research done by the Environmental Defense Fund and other members of the Paper Task Force who study the environmental impacts of the paper industry.

For more information on this environmental benefits statement, or to inquire about environmentally friendly papers, please contact New Leaf Paper – info@newleafpaper.com Tel: 888 • 989 • 5323.

For a full list of NSP's titles, please call **1-800-567-6772** *or check out our website at:*

www.newsociety.com

NEW SOCIETY PUBLISHERS